EDITORS, PUBLISHERS
AND NEWSPAPER ETHICS

EDITORS PUBLISHERS AND NEWSPAPER ETHICS

A report to the American Society
of Newspaper Editors

Philip Meyer

American Society of Newspaper Editors

April, 1983

American Society of Newspaper Editors
The Newspaper Center
P.O. Box 17004
Washington, D.C. 20041

ISBN: 0-943-086-02-7
LCC Card No: 83-71452

Contents

Contents

Foreword

Editors and reporters have talked ethics endlessly. Scarcely a day goes by that objectivity, fairness, balance or some other ethical question does not arise in the newsroom. Did the reporter write a bad story? Did an editor make a bad call? Unless advertising or a publisher's pet interest is involved, publishers are usually left out of the discussions. Many editors prefer separation of church and state and make clear that the church is the news department because editors and reporters are closer to God.

Yet there is no escaping the fact that the greatest power in a newspaper is wielded by the publisher. Decisions he or she makes often set the tone of the newspaper. Anyone interested in newspaper ethics ought to look at the publishers and their relationship with editors. That is what the Ethics Committee of the American Society of Newspaper Editors asked Philip Meyer, William Rand Kenan Jr. Professor of Journalism at the University of North Carolina at Chapel Hill, to do.

Phil has done a remarkable job, as would be expected of the author of *Precision Journalism*, the valuable handbook on the use of statistical methods in reporting and a former reporter and corporate executive with the Knight-Ridder Newspapers. As Frank McCulloch, Executive Editor of the McClatchy Newspapers, put it after reading the first draft of the report:

"Phil Meyer and his colleagues have produced—and this despite my aversion for hyperbolic adjectives—a monumental work. Full digestion is going to take months, but even at this early stage, I think it's clear they have earned our full attention."

Other members of the Ethics Committee who read the report and commented before the deadline for publication used the word "fascinating."

Bob Schulman, an outside member of the committee who is media commentator for WHAS-TV in Louisville, was one. He saw the report as having "great potential for stimulating rethinking and encouraging valuable changes in the process of press decision-making—provided that the report is not just dropped into the journalistic stream." Specifically, he urged that the Ethics Committee draw up detailed proposals "for interpretation, widespread consideration and application."

To Bill Heine, Editor of London, Ont., Free Press, the report's findings were "fascinating" largely because "they reflect what I have considered to be the way the newspaper world is. Publishers, editors and staff largely agree on most aspects of the field. The differences are those of emphasis rather than strong disagreements."

Gerald Warren, Editor of the San Diego Union, also viewed the report as confirming many of his beliefs. In particular he thought it logical that editors follow instinct in reaching most ethical decisions while many publishers rely on printed rules.

It is important to point out that while the report is drawing wide praise, it does not carry a stamp of approval or disapproval of the ASNE Ethics Committee. The report was prepared for the committee but its findings and proposals are Phil Meyer's alone. In fact, some of the proposals are vigorously opposed. For example, the suggestion that newspapers establish ethics committees made up of representatives of all departments—not just the newsroom—is considered dangerous by a number of editors.

Robert H. Wills, Editor of the Milwakee Sentinel, was quite emphatic:

"I am of the old fashioned school that believes a barrier should remain between the editorial and the business sides of newspapers if we are to be true to our readers. There must be recognition that we confront different problems in different ways.

"For that reason, when Philip Meyer reached the conclusion that it is perhaps time for a company-wide code of ethics, I was brought up short. Given the same set of findings from the survey, I do not arrive at the same conclusion.

"If the business side of the operation wants to have a code of ethics for dealing with its advertisers and in its other business decisions, that's fine with me. I'm sure our company has such informal ethics and principles which guide its business dealings.

"And if the editorial side wants to have its code of ethics to deal with problems of communication with the readers, that's also fine with me. On my newspaper there is an editorial code of ethics, published quarterly so our readers are aware of it.

"But I am not so sure that the thinking that determines the profits of the newspaper operation should be the thinking that is used in editorial decisions, and vice versa. In fact, I am sure the thinking should be different to reflect the different goals. It follows that any codes also should be different.

"Therefore, I wish to make it clear that while I support the survey and its findings, I do not support the conclusions of the report. Those are conclusions of Philip Meyer and his associates."

One can go even further and insist that such committees would lead to compromising of principles that would set back the struggle to raise newspaper standards. Advertising managers would be right back in the newsrooms. Moreover, Phil would have such committees write codes of ethics, a strange suggestion in view of his conclusion that the best publishers are those that take an active interest in the news operation and that "the idea of codifying ethical principles, while popular overall, is most accepted among publishers who are least likely to get their hands dirty with real-life application of those codes."

William F. Thomas, editor and executive vice president of the Los Angeles Times, although "impressed" by the study, noted "two tiny quibbles:

"One. Meyer notes that younger editors of large papers are more likely to take a restrained approach to publication of stories than older editors. He ascribes this—'perhaps'—to the scar tissue on older editors. Room for argument here, I would think. Experience seems to me the more likely influencing factor, not toughness of mind. All editors learn sooner or later that decisions not to publish can create problems from many directions—internal and external—unless they are based on pretty firm and clearly understood grounds.

"Two. A little later in the study, we get into the ethical situations involving money. Meyer theorizes that the tough 'anti-money' stance characterized here is really a reflection of the old editorial-business side antipathy. I think it more likely that the answer is simpler, that what is reflected is just a recognition that in situations involving something of value, money is the greatest and most easily recognized corrupter."

Katherine Fanning, who serves as both editor and publisher of the Anchorage Daily News and vice-chairman of the ASNE Ethics Committee, expressed concern about the methodology of the survey—a doubt she voiced midway in the work.

"I remain somewhat troubled by the circulation weighting system he employed which has the effect of counting a large newspaper editor or publisher's opinion equal to that of ten or fifteen smaller newspaper people. The generalization, for example, about the editor/publisher arrangements that work best is primarily dictated by what works best at a *large newspaper.*"

Mrs. Fanning valued the study "not so much for what it reveals about editor/publisher relationships (except that they are not at war contrary to popular belief) but for what Meyer concludes about changing values." She added:

"I particularly liked his analysis of the internal and external forces impacting newspeople's ethical decisions and the distinctions implied between larger newspapers where a distance can be maintained between the paper and events, and smaller papers which are necessarily closer to the community. The clash between the internal pressures of community expectations about a newspaper's role in promoting civic betterment depicts a very real dilemma acutely felt by newspaper people from smaller cities. And it may even strike at the heart of public disenchantment with the press. 'Can rigid application of traditional journalistic ethics be relaxed without inviting the very evils they were formed to ward off?'"

Like Frank McCulloch, Bob Schulman, Bill Heine, Bob Wills, and others, Mrs. Fanning urged that ways be found to continue discussion of the issues raised in the Meyer report, asking:

"Can a new ethic, which calls for more thoughtful analysis of individual cases and fewer knee-jerk responses be formed?"

Calling for "an important new ethical debate," Mrs. Fanning pointed out:

"The finding that editors want more publisher involvement in the newsroom will evoke howls in some quarters as will the finding that editors should participate more in business decisions. Meyer's conclusion that there is a prevailing trend toward 'ethical wholeness' within a united rather than divided newspaper could provide fodder for some lively discussion."

> Robert H. Phelps
> Chairman
> Ethics Committee
> American Society of Newspaper Editors

April 1983

How This Survey Was Done

This is a study about the relationships of editors and publishers and how they work together to set and enforce ethical standards on daily newspapers. As its practitioners know, the newspaper business is complicated. Any plan to study it must be complicated, too, and the investigator who fails to define terms and establish clear procedures risks drowning in ambiguity. This study counts and measures things, and it is meant to be replicable. If this good intention is realized, the study's procedures should be so clear and its interpretations so sharply defined that some future investigator could take the same steps, ask the same questions, and know from the results whether or not the industry had changed in the intervening time.

Two design issues had to be resolved at the beginning. One was the very basic question of to whom or what the results should be generalized. The other was the procedural issue of how to define the main actors in the study. The first problem was aggravated by the tremendous variation in newspaper size and a resulting paradox: the vast majority of newspapers are relatively small, i.e. under 50,000 daily circulation, but the majority of newspaper readers are served by the larger papers. Two percent of the newspapers (the 31 with circulation over 250,000) account for about a quarter of the total daily circulation in the United States.

If this study were primarily concerned with making life easier for editors and publishers, it would be fashioned so that newspapers in general were the population under study, and it would be based on a representative sample of them, with smaller papers constituting the great bulk of the units in the sample, just as they do in real life. If, on the other hand, the study is to be concerned with social responsibilities, it is readers, not newspapers, that need to be equally represented.

The latter option was chosen in this case. Newspapers were chosen for study at random—but with the probability of selection made proportionate to the size of their daily circulation. The sample is therefore representative of the population of newspaper users. It is as though we had taken a pure random sample of persons who buy newspapers, either by subscription or single copy, asked them what papers they read, and selected those papers into our study.

The execution of this process was easier than it sounds. Statisticians at the Research Triangle Institute used a computer to examine the circulation numbers in the 1981 Editor & Publisher Yearbook and determined that the desired sample size of 333 newspapers could be obtained by choosing the paper represented by approximately every 140,000th newspaper buyer. Imagine the total paid press runs of all the daily newspapers on an average day in 1981 piled in a single stack. Now, from a random start somewhere among the first 140,000, peel them off one at a time and set aside every 140,000th paper. Those are the newspapers in our sample.

One other step is necessary, however, to make these 333 newspapers truly representative of all newspaper buyers. Some are so large that their selection is automatic, and some of the very largest will be selected more than once. To complete the requirement of equal representation for all consumers of daily newspapers, it is necessary to count these extra large newspapers more than once—in proportion to their size. This task was accomplished by the simple means of duplicating responses from those newspapers enough times to give them their proportional weight.

The numbers in this survey are therefore circulation-adjusted whenever they refer to editors, publishers, or staff members. When they refer to readers, they are simple projections to all daily newspaper readers in the United States—with circulation used as a universal indicator of readership. Aside from giving readers their just recognition with this procedure, the method has the effect of producing very powerful generalizations. The news people responding to this survey represent more than half of all daily circulation in the United States. As a result, sampling error is quite small—and representativeness quite good—for editors and publishers. For staff members, however, the numbers are only crudely representative. This difference occurs because an editor or a publisher represents himself or herself. Chance plays no part in the selection once the newspaper is chosen. A single staff member, on the other hand, represents all of the diversity of the staff at his or her newspaper, and that selection is subject to chance. The problem is probably minor when the whole population of newspaper readers is considered, but it may not be so minor when only parts of that population are examined. This report therefore considers staff attitudes in less detail than those of editors and publishers.

Even though this study is reader-oriented rather than editor- or publisher- oriented, the actual number of newspapers behind each of the main categories of response is reported in the appendix so that you can check if you ever suspect that an unexpected result is too thinly supported by real life.

The second major problem, defining the actors in the study, is solved more straightforwardly. Because this is a study about editors and publishers, we must make very clear at the outset what we mean by the terms "editor" and "publisher." Again, in the interests of replicability, we must make the definitions so clear that another researcher could follow them and come out in the same place.

It was evident from the start that titles in the newspaper business are too variable and ambiguous to be of much help. It was more important to keep functions rather than titles uniform. Our procedure, therefore, began with the editor. For the purpose of this study, the editor was defined as the highest-ranking person with full-time responsibility for the news operation at the paper. This definition held regardless of title, and it prevented an editor-publisher from being defined as the editor. It also ruled out the selection of editors whose only responsibility was the editorial page. A person who was the top editor of two papers had his responses counted twice in the few cases where both papers fell into the sample.

Finding the person to define as publisher was fairly easy once the editor had been identified. The publisher, in this study, is that person to whom the highest-ranking editor reports. If an editor found the concept of "reporting" ambiguous—and some did—he or she was asked who did the hiring, firing, salary adjustment, and budget approval for the editor. In certain group situations, that person was a corporate officer in some other city, but was nevertheless defined as the publisher. An editor-publisher was defined as the publisher if he or she was the person to whom the highest-ranking full-time editor reported. Anyone who was the publisher of more than one paper in the sample had his or her responses counted for each of those papers.

Selection of a person to represent the staff at each newspaper was done as randomly as possible but still kept within a fairly limited range of writers, desk people, and lower management. Seven job descriptions were written and rotated so that each editor was asked to match a staff name to a randomly selected position. This provided the researchers with staff names without their selection being left entirely to the editors. If more than one person fit the description, the full list was obtained, and selection made according to alphabetical order.

Data were collected in two stages. Editors were contacted by telephone and their eligibility verified. Once this was done, the editor was asked questions to establish the identity of the publisher and the eligible staff person. Some substantive questions on the frequency of certain kinds of ethical problems were also asked at this stage. A follow-up self-administered form was then sent to the editor, his or her publisher, and a staff member at each newspaper.

xiv**How This Survey Was Done**

Response rates were quite high for a survey of any type, much less a complicated, two-stage, mail-and-telephone procedure. Fully 97.6 percent of the editors (325 our of 333) supplied data for the first stage. Six editors refused and two were dropped from the sample because their newspapers closed while the study was in progress. Raw response rates for the mail survey, based on the 331 newspapers still in the sample, were 78.2 percent for editors, 71 percent for publishers, and 72.5 percent for staff members. Only 22 of the 331 newspapers produced no response from any of the three persons contacted.

Field work for this project was performed by the Research Triangle Institute of North Carolina under the supervision of Don Jackson, project director, and Jennifer J. McNeill, survey specialist. James R. Chromy supervised the sampling. J. Walker Smith, School of Journalism, University of North Carolina at Chapel Hill, managed the data file, searched the literature and checked the facts. This project was conceived and supervised by the Ethics Committee of the American Society of Newspaper Editors under the chairmanship of Robert E. Phelps of the Boston Globe.

Others who offered helpful advice include Robert L. Burke, Malcolm F. Mallette, Carol Reuss and Donald Shaw. The project was financed by the John and Mary R. Markle Foundation. All errors, careless interpretations, and non sequiters are the sole responsibility of the author.

Philip Meyer
William Rand Kenan Jr. Professor
School of Journalism
University of North Carolina at Chapel Hill

Introduction

The newspaper editors, publishers and staff members questioned in this survey were asked a group of anecdotal questions about ethical problems of the sort sometimes encountered in the newspaper business. For a quick overview of their content, you can turn to page 68 and scan the questions and the distribution of responses.

While the list is fascinating, its validity as a guide to contemporary ethical practices is open to question. Choices that are easy to make when the questions are hypothetical may be made less often when the problems and the consequences of the choices are real. Fortunately, it was not the purpose of this survey to put specific ethical questions to a popular vote. Instead, it was designed to measure some underlying attitudes and to find out how editors and publishers work together—or separately—to set the ethical tone and practice of a newspaper. The question is not the sort that can be asked directly because self-awareness does not come easily in an area as sensitive as this. And so the patterns and structures formed by the responses are at least as important as the responses themselves. This report examines the patterns in the following order:

1. *Agreement and disagreement between editor and publisher*: One of the first things to establish is the degree to which the two groups approach ethical problems with common or differing perspectives. The way to do it is to compare their responses to individual question items.

2. *Staff attitudes*: The ethical standards of management are of little significance if they are not executed at the staff level. So we need to know how closely staff values fit those of the folks who run the place.

3. *The underlying publisher-editor relationship*: Some publishers never go near the newsroom. Others are seen there all the time. To get very far in our quest, we need to classify the basic nature of the relationship. When that is done, we can see how it affects ethical outcomes.

4. *A catalog of ethical problems*: Making a list is only the first step. The important thing is to see how certain responses cluster together, revealing underlying patterns that provide clues to how the decisions are made.

5. *How the formation of ethical values varies with different kinds of editor-publisher relationships*: At last, we get to the heart of the matter

and begin to look for those operating styles that seem to go hand in hand with what we might describe as "ethical efficiency."

6. *The ethically efficient newspaper*: The report concludes with some speculation about the arrangements that seem to work best and what newspaper managers might do to improve the ethical efficiency of their own operations.

PART ONE

Editors, Publishers, and Ethical Issues

Editors and publishers tend to see eye-to-eye on the substance of most ethical issues.

They are much less likely to agree on the procedures for resolving those issues or even on who at the newspaper should take part in that resolution. They generally have very different ideas on where one's ethical turf ends and the other's begins. These differences are kept mostly harmless through a time-honored, although unconscious, technique for avoiding conflict: misperception of what is really going on.

This study, based on information collected from editors, publishers, and staff members, has no way of comparing the reported perceptions of either group with reality. It can only report that they see the same things in different ways. The most striking specific example turned up in the survey involves the work of screen writer and former editor Kurt Luedtke which sparked some of the current debate about newspaper ethics, "Absence of Malice." The film has been seen by editors and publishers representing more than half the newspaper circulation in the country. At some newspapers, accounting for eight to nine percent of total circulation, formal action was taken in response to Luedtke's drama: discussion groups, committees, or other activities to put ethics on the newspaper's policy agenda.

On that subject, there was agreement. On the subject of who took the initiative to start that response, there was virtually no agreement. Editors, overwhelmingly, thought they had made the move. Publishers, by a margin of nearly two-to-one, were sure they had done it.

A good manager, of course, motivates subordinates with such subtlety and finesse that the subordinate often sincerely believes that the manager's ideas are his or her own. Any worker will carry out policies with greater energy and enthusiasm when he or she has had a role in originating those policies. But the differences in editors' and publishers' perceptions go far beyond such subjective judgments as who was first to get a good idea. The differences involve objective reality as well.

Take a simple, easily quantifiable activity: the number of times the publisher walks into the newsroom. Not much room for ambiguity there. The publisher is either present or not. Nevertheless, publishers see themselves as physically present in the newsroom far more often than editors admit to being aware of that presence. The great preponderance of publishers, accounting for 73 percent of daily circulation, report walking into the newsroom more than once a week. Awareness of that presence is much less among editors (48 percent of circulation) and staff members (44 percent).

Perhaps publishers' visits to the newsroom are perfunctory and brief. One imagines the publisher entering on tiptoe, glancing around for reassurance that all is proceeding normally, and then slipping out before being noticed by the busy editor and the staff. Is it possible?

Not according to the publishers. They tend to see themselves as far more active in the news operation than do editors. How often, survey participants were asked, does the publisher order a major investigation or series of articles on a specific subject? "Never," according to most editors (61 percent of circulation). But only a minority of publishers (45 percent of circulation) agreed.

More is going on here than wishful thinking or ego building. Editors and publishers genuinely disagree on where one's turf should end and the other's begin. Publishers want some overlap. Editors prefer fences with themselves on one side and the publishers on the other.

The main body of the survey asked for choices among different responses to some hypothetical, but not altogether unreal, ethical dilemmas. Some of these questions were followed up with queries about who, the editor or the publisher or both, should play the main role in solving the problem. Other questions asked more generally about the ideal working relationship between editor and publisher.

The bottom line: on most substantive ethical problems, you can take a vote among the nation's editors or the nation's publishers and come out with about the same answers. On most questions involving turf, you'll get bigger differences.

One question sums the turf issue:

Newspapers vary greatly in the amount of involvement that publishers have in the news operations. Here are four statements describing different levels of publisher involvement. Regardless of how things work at your paper, which of the following statements comes closest to describing the way you think publishers *ought to operate:*

1. The publisher should always be involved in deciding what appears in his or her newspaper on a day-to-day basis.

2. The publisher should generally be involved in deciding what appears in his or her newspaper over the long run, but not on a daily basis.

3. The publisher should be involved in hiring good people to run the news operation, but not in deciding what appears in the paper; his only intervention in the news operation should be to hire or fire the editor.

4. The publisher should have nothing whatever to do with the news operation.

Editors, publishers, and staff members alike overwhelmingly rejected the extreme alternatives in favor of the middle two. And the second —that the publisher should have general involvement, but not on a daily basis, was the consensus across all three groups. But there were strong minorities among editors (41 percent of circulation) and staff (45 percent) for keeping the publisher further on his own side of the fence. The rate of publisher agreement with those minorities was only 18 percent.

These differences persisted through several variant question wordings. Few publishers and virtually no editors want the publisher to "be the boss all the way," as one of the question items put it. And the notion that the publisher should not give orders to the editor under any circumstances is not widely held. It is, however, twice as frequent among editors as it is among publishers (26 percent of circulation to 11 percent), and the frequency triples when only staff members (36 percent) are examined.

This difference is found in a specific application. Those surveyed were asked to agree or disagree with the statement, "When there is disagreement between editor and publisher over the endorsement of a political candidate, the editor should have the final say." The consensus answer is to disagree, but there were substantial minorities in favor of letting the editor come out on top in such a struggle. Publishers with this view represented 22 percent of circulation, compared to 37 percent for the editors and 47 percent for the staff members.

When the problems posed get still more specific, this difference of view persists. One of the questions dealt with the not infrequent problem of a local reporter getting uncomfortably close to his sources:

Your paper's city hall reporter has gotten so close to the mayor and his staff that they frequently consult him before making major decisions. Should the editor:

1. Fire the reporter.

2. Move the reporter to a different beat.

3. Admonish the reporter to maintain a reasonable distance from his sources.

4. Reward the reporter for developing such a good knowledge of his subject and such loyal sources.

Editors and publishers were in fairly close agreement on the substance of this issue, with close to two out of three in each group choosing the moderate course of admonition over more vigorous measures. Where they parted company was on the question of who should be involved in making that uncontroversial decision. Editors representing 86 percent of the circulation and publishers with only 49 percent felt that the editor alone should make that decision. Staff members, not unexpectedly, sided with the editors.

Another question involving staff behavior produced a similar pattern. The question asked what should be done about an investigative reporter who uses a computer to analyze criminal court records and produce a prize-winning series—and then receives an offer from a computer manufacturer to describe his methods at a seminar for a $500 fee. Editors and publishers split along nearly identical lines, with the most favored choice being to let the reporter make the speech, but bar him from accepting an honorarium (staff members were more likely than either editors or publishers to approve the fee). The similarity was striking:

	Publishers	*Editors*
Make the speech, keep the money:	28%	24%
Have money paid through university:	19	18
Make the speech, reject the money:	48	51
Don't make the speech:	5	8

But harmony evaporates when the issue of who should make that decision is argued. Most editors, representing 72 percent of circulation, said the editor alone should decide that issue. Among publishers, it was 37 percent.

These two examples involve staff behavior, and it could be argued that any kind of organization would find such conflicts in the chain of command, with superiors and subordinates disagreeing on the amount of delegation which is appropriate. We therefore turn next to an example which goes to the heart of the editor's function: deciding what to put in or leave out of the newspaper. Like most of the questions in the survey, it is not an easy one:

A prominent citizen is vacationing alone in Key West, and his hotel burns down. The wire service story lists him among those who escaped uninjured and identifies the hotel as a popular gathering place for affluent gays. The citizen says he'll commit suicide if you publish his name in the story. Should the editor:

1. *Publish the story in full.*
2. *Publish the story, but without mentioning the gay angle.*
3. *Publish the story, but without mentioning the local citizen.*
4. *Kill the story.*

Virtually no one wanted to kill the story. Editors and publishers divided in nearly identical patterns over whether to publish the story in full (the choice of about four out of 10 in both groups), and publishing the story without the gay angle (the choice of half). But once again, editors were far more insistent (60 percent to 39 percent) than publishers that this decision is the editor's alone to make.

If editors and publishers are in so much agreement on matters of substance, does it matter that there is disagreement over procedure and editorial prerogative? Perhaps not. The healthiest outcome might indeed be mutual misperception, with both editors and publishers believing that they are the centers of power when it comes to deciding these questions. As long as the questions lead to the same answers, the ambiguous location of the power is not likely to be noticed, nor will either side's autonomy be questioned. However, there are some compelling circumstances which operate to keep us from letting it go at that.

For one thing, the agreement of which we speak involves editors and publishers as groups. As individuals, editors and publishers are likely to clash on individual issues even where their respective groups show similar distributions of belief. If half the editors and half the publishers in the nation each embraces philosophy X while the other half of each group prefers philosophy Y, we can say that editors and publishers think much alike as groups, but that will not help those papers where random fate has paired a philosophy X editor with a Y publisher. Of course, more than chance governs these pairings, and like-minded editors and publishers tend to seek each other out. Nevertheless, mismatches will occur.

Secondly, there are some substantive issues where the general pattern of parallels between editor thinking and publisher belief does not prevail. When editors and publishers as groups differ sharply on substantive ethics, the difference of opinion over procedure is no longer an academic matter.

Substantive disagreement between editors as a whole and publishers as a whole therefore deserves careful examination despite the fact that it is found in only a minority of issues. What these issues have in common is not some overriding moral philosophy so much as a matter of style and visceral reaction to certain kinds of problems. Specifically, editors and publishers appear to be at their greatest overall disagreement when the issue involves money and its uses.

Of the 22 anecdotal dilemmas posed in the survey, only three sharply separated editors and publishers. Money was directly involved in two of these problems and indirectly in the third.

The sharpest substantive disagreement between editors and publishers comes in response to the following anecdote, which appeared in the survey instrument with a slight misprint (corrected here in parenthesis):

Your company receives a special rate from a major hotel chain for your traveling employees. A staff member goes out of town for a three-day business meeting and, because the site of the meeting is a major cultural center, decides to stay through the week(end) at his own expense. He pays his own hotel bill for Friday and Saturday nights, but at the special commercial rate. Your company has a conflict-of-interest policy against employees accepting any kind of favor or reward from suppliers. Should your company:

1. Fire the traveling employee.

2. Require him to reimburse the hotel for the difference between the commercial and regular rate and warn him not to repeat the practice.

3. Warn him not to repeat the practice, but not worry about reimbursement because the amount is so small.

4. Make a ruling that such discounts are not considered favors or rewards under the conflict-of-interest policy.

The number of news people whose ethical sensibilities are offended by the reporter's action in this case strains credulity. Fortunately, as noted earlier, we are less concerned with absolute numbers than the differences among groups.

Editors were far less willing (and staff members even less so) than publishers to let the employee have his cut-rate weekend. Those wanting the employee to reimburse the hotel and abandon the practice included, after adjustment for circulation, 24 percent of the publishers, 44 percent of the editors, and 65 percent of the staff.

What accounts for the differences? Ghosts of the old editorial-business office conflict may be haunting us here. News-editorial people tend to be suspicious of money and its power, while a publisher is more likely to evaluate expenditures in instrumental terms: money is a tool, and one uses it as efficiently as one can. The hotel chain's discount is made to attract a large-volume customer, and it doesn't care whether the lodgers it brings in are on their own errands or the company's. The publisher may perceive the transaction as a fringe benefit which costs the company nothing, and which the employees might as well share. Do the editors fear that the employee will be inclined to write favorably about the hotel chain if he pays the corporate rate himself for a visit on his own time, but not be so affected if he is there on the company's time and money? Perhaps. But the responses of editors to other questions in this survey suggest that a more gut-level process is at stake. News people tend to bristle at the smell of money. This reaction arose in several forms.

Money was involved in the substantive case with the next highest level of disagreement between publishers and editors as groups. In this case, the survey author's intent to keep all the examples fictitious came perilously close to being defeated:

Some newspaper companies in Florida donated money to a campaign to defeat a statewide referendum which, if passed, would have legalized gambling. Which of the following statements comes closest to your view on this action?

1. A newspaper that takes an editorial stand on an issue has a right, and possibly even a duty, to back up its belief with its money.

2. The contributions are justified if the referendum would have a detrimental effect on the business climate in which the newspaper operates.

3. The contributions should not have been made because they might lead readers to question the objectivity of the papers' news coverage.

4. No political contributions should ever be made by newspapers; the news and editorial columns make us powerful enough already, and adding money only indicates inappropriate hunger for more power.

Something of the sort did, of course, happen in Florida in 1978 and became the subject of an investigation by the National News Council (Columbia Journalism Review, March/April, 1979). It was not, however, the intention of this survey to pose a referendum on anyone's real-life ethical problem, and so we were relieved to receive a communication from a Florida news person asserting that the four alternatives listed above were nothing at all like the real-life choices. Good. The fiction is difficult enough.

Publishers representing 33 percent of circulation, compared to only 13 per cent for editors, said the contributions could be justified (choices 1 and 2). Staff members were slightly more opposed to the contributions than the editors. A majority of all three groups opposed the donations (choices 3 and 4), but the fact that it was a smaller majority for publishers reaffirms the point that publishers are less squeamish about money.

One other substantive question in the survey divided editors and publishers in a significant way, and this time the money connection was not so apparent.

The restaurant reviewer at your paper has become friendly with a local restaurant operator and, working without pay, has helped his friend to design and plan a new restaurant with a continental theme — the exact sort of restaurant whose absence in your town he has decried in his column. Should the editor:
  1. Fire the restaurant critic.
  2. Admonish the critic not to get so close to sources, and ban any mention of the new restaurant in his column.
  3. Advise the critic not to do it again, but take no further action.
  4. Do nothing.

Editors are much more ready than publishers to go after that restaurant critic. Staff members, for a change, react more like the publishers. Among the publishers, those with 48 percent of circulation would settle for none or mild action compared to only 30 percent for editors. This is a reverse variant of economic conflict of interest; the economic good, expert advice, is flowing to the businessman, not the reporter. The editor, perhaps, is more likely than others to expect something to flow back. He is certainly less ready to tolerate a close connection between a news-side functionary and an advertiser. These data do not tell us what different forces motivate editor and publisher. They do tell us one revealing thing: newspaper people in general tend to be guided by economic connections in making ethical judgments. The tendency shows itself in several different ways, and some of them will be examined later in this report.

In general, there appears to be a fairly close correspondence between what editors and publishers believe to be the ideal relationship and the relationship which actually exists. Most think, as has been noted, that the publisher should be generally involved in deciding what appears in the paper in the long run, but not on a daily basis. And most say that is what happens on their papers. In another area, however, both editors and publishers perceive a gap between the ideal and the reality. That's the bad news. The good news is that they agree on what the reality should be.

Both sides want to move editors toward greater involvement in financial planning and marketing decisions. The marketing approach and the notion of the total newspaper are still relatively new concepts, and, although widely accepted, they are not as widely implemented as they could be. Both concepts involve making the editor less insulated from the reality that a newspaper is a business and exposing him more to the opportunities and constraints inherent in business operations. The attitude was tapped with this question:

One issue in some companies is how much editors should be involved in the company's marketing and financial plans. Which of the following statements best describes the role you think the editor should have at your company:

1. The editor should participate fully in financial planning and marketing decisions.

2. The editor should be kept fully informed in financial planning and marketing decisions, but should participate only when questions relating to his specific expertise are involved.

3. The editor should be kept informed of financial planning and marketing decisions on a "need-to-know" basis, i.e. whenever his help is needed in carrying out the decisions.

4. The editor should be kept insulated from all financial planning and marketing decisions so that he can concentrate on putting out the paper.

A decade ago, the latter two choices would probably have been the norm as news and business sides, like church and state, were bounded by a wall of separation. In this survey, a plurality of both editors and publishers vote for full participation by editors in financial planning and marketing decisions. Staff opinion remains more traditional: most would limit the editor's participation to questions involving his specific expertise.

Publishers and editors alike find that their ideal of full editor involvement is not often met. Editor participation is most often limited to situations where editorial expertise is needed or where the editor's help is needed in carrying out decisions. The comparison (based on readers):

	Publishers		Editors	
	Ideal	Reality	Ideal	Reality
1. Full editor participation	42%	27%	45%	28%
2. When expertise needed	34	38	39	33
3. When "need to know" exists	23	34	14	35
4. Keep editor insulated	1	1	2	4

If editors have failed to press for fuller participation because they thought their publishers opposed it, or if publishers have maintained the status quo in presumed deference to editors' desires, these numbers suggest a need for reassessment. And they leave room for conjecture about the effect of greater business involvement by editors on ethical values. If the few differences between editors and publishers in ethical judgments are conditioned by different attitudes toward money, and if these attitudes are the result of different levels of business experience, exposing editors to that experience might lead to a convergence of values. Before we can guess where that might lead, we must first look at existing values in more detail.

PART TWO

Ethics at the Staff Level

Ethical views among newspaper staffs parallel those of the editors in most cases, but there are some notable exceptions, some of them stemming from a difference in perception.

The staff, for example, is much more likely than the editor to see the publisher as a malign influence in the newsroom. More than a value judgment is involved here. Certain kinds of behavior are perceived more often by the staff than by the editor, and our data do not tell us who is right. The biggest difference came on this question:

How often, according to your best estimate, does the publisher of your paper ask for special handling of an article about a company or organization which has some economic clout over your newspaper?

Publishers with 58 percent of the readership, compared to 54 percent for editors and only 32 percent for the staff said such a thing *never* happened. Among editors and publishers who said it did happen, the most often cited frequency was about once or twice a year. Staff members were more likely to say it happened several times a year.

A similar result was obtained when the question was asked about special handling for organizations or individuals with whom the publisher had strong social ties. Staff members were far more likely than editors or publishers to say it happened at all, and they perceived greater frequency if it did happen.

Some of this difference in perception may come from a simple disagreement over what constitutes legitimate intervention. The staff, in general, is much less willing to recognize a publisher's prerogatives than is the editor. The wall of separation is still very real to newspaper staffers, and publisher intervention in the editorial side is more likely to be viewed as a transgression by the staff than it is by the editor. Thus the staff appears as a conservative force in the survey. For example, 47 percent of the staff (circulation-adjusted) believes the editor and not the publisher should have the final say in a showdown over endorsement of a political candidate. Only 37 percent of the editors (and 22 percent of the publishers) feel that way. The staff has greater resistance to the total newspaper concept, with four out of five opposing full participation for the editor in financial planning and marketing decisions.

The following question shows clearly how staff perception of the publisher's role differs from that of both editor and publisher:

The publisher is convinced that a downtown amusement park is just what the community needs. The editor of the editorial page opposes it. Should the publisher:
1. *Order the editor to support the amusement park.*
2. *Drop some gentle hints to the editor, but avoid a direct order.*
3. *Avoid discussing the issue with the editor at all.*
4. *Encourage the editor to call the issue as he sees it.*

Staff members were overwhelmingly (68 percent of circulation) in favor of the publisher keeping hands off, either not discussing the issue with the editor at all or, if he does discuss it, encouraging the editor to call it as he or she sees it. Only 52 percent of the editors and 38 percent of the publishers were in favor of such publisher restraint.

Does the staff believe that publishers are in fact that restrained? No. The staff is somewhat more likely to perceive a strong publisher, one who is "the boss, all the way," than either the editor or the publisher himself. The subtleties of power relationships may be more difficult to appreciate at the staff level. Finally, staff hostility to the total newspaper concept may be linked to the perception that the concept violates the model of separation. The staff shows significant resistance to a marketing or financial role for the editor, with four out of five opposed to giving him or her full participation in those decisions.

On substantive issues, the staff divergences from editors' views tend to follow a hard-line devotion to traditional values. Going to jail to protect the confidentiality of a source is twice as attractive to a staff person—who is more likely to be the person in jail—than it is to an editor or publisher. A hard line on such protection for sources "even if it means a long jail term for the reporter and heavy financial cost to the newspaper" was taken by publishers representing 18 percent of circulation, compared to 20 percent for editors and 40 percent for the staff people.

An anecdotal question about an investigative reporter who turns up information which, if revealed, would result in a financial loss to himself drew responses from the staff that were more sympathetic to the reporter than were those of editors or publishers. The issue posed was:

An investigative reporter does a thorough and praiseworthy expose of inequalities in tax assessment practices. In the course of investigating for the story, he looks at his own assessment records and finds that a value-enhancing addition to his property was never recorded, and as a result, his taxes are $300 less than they should be. He reports this fact in the first draft of his story, but later, at the urging of his wife, takes it out: Should the editor:

1. Insist that he leave the information in, even though it will raise the reporter's taxes.

2. Talk to the wife and try to persuade her that the reporter's honesty at leaving it in will be rewarded, someday.

3. Leave it to the reporter to decide, but appeal to his conscience.

4. Don't interfere.

The consensus across all groups was that the information should be left in, but staffers were well short of unanimity. Those taking this view represented 58 percent of circulation, compared to 74 percent for the editors and 63 percent for publishers.

Financial self-interest may not be the relevant aim here so much as a desire for freedom from editorial dictates on what to put in or leave out of a story. On another question involving economic self-interest, the case of the reporter who stays in a hotel on his own time at a corporate discount drew a much harsher reaction from the staff than from either editors or publishers. Sixty-five percent of the staff, but only 44 percent of the editors wanted the reporter to pay the hotel the difference between the regular rate and the newspaper's special corporate rate.

Professional self-interest operates quite clearly in another area. The staff is less interested in accepting ethical constraints on news-gathering methods than are editors. This issue examined in this category involves concealment of the reporter's own strongly held views in order to gain the cooperation of news sources who hold contrasting views. Editors were twice as likely as the staff members to favor bypassing that problem by assigning someone else to the story. Staff members were more likely (by 82 to 65 percent) to let the reporter keep quiet about his views or even pose as a sympathetic neutral in order to get the needed cooperation.

On questions dealing with self-imposed restraints on publication, staff members are more likely than editors to adopt a full-speed-ahead, damn-the-torpedoes stance. Most news people would rather publish than not, and it is usual to decide a close call by coming down on the side of publishing. This is an easier rule to follow, however, the more one is removed from having to think about the consequences. Staff members were three times as likely as publishers and half again as likely as editors to believe that leaked grand jury information should be published "whenever the material is newsworthy." And an anecdotal question about self-restraint to reduce the harrassment for a newsworthy refugee family drew far less support from the staff than from either the editor or the publisher. Staff views tend to follow traditional newsroom values with fewer qualifications or reservations than are expressed by news people with greater responsibility.

PART THREE

Publisher Participation: Four Styles

Whether publishers and editors agree or disagree on ethical questions is a moot point if the publisher does not participate in the editorial direction of the newspaper. It therefore makes sense to try to classify the different participatory styles of newspaper publishers and then see how those styles relate to ethical outcomes. A number of questions in the survey asked about the frequency of different kinds of publisher participation.

Some of these questions were deliberately framed to identify what might be described from the editor's point of view as benign participation —acts that are helpful to an editor and whose motivation is to improve the quality of the news-editorial product. Other questions asked about participation that is relatively malign from the editor's viewpoint—obtaining special treatment for friends or for advertisers or using the newsroom for personal benefit.

A comparative evaluation of publishers along these lines can be made with considerable accuracy when a number of question items are combined to form an index. Combining items in this way reduces the risk of error because no classification depends entirely on the response to a single question. Items for such an index must be intercorrelated. In other words, if one item tells enough about a person so that it predicts with a fair amount of accuracy how that person will score on a second item, the two items are probably measuring the same underlying trait.

A computer-aided search of the question items describing publisher behavior produced two sets which met this test. Items in the first set point to productive publisher intervention—productive in the sense that editors would generally welcome it—and they meet the test of intercorrelation. So each publisher was given one point on a four-point scale for each of the following responses:

1. The publisher suggests a major investigation or series of articles

but leaves the final decision to the editor (at least once or twice a year).

2. The publisher demonstrates, by selective use of praise or criticism, what he wants the editor to do (at least once or twice a year).

3. The publisher walks into the newsroom (at least nearly every week).

4. The publisher questions or otherwise participates in the assignment of a particular reporter to a story or beat (any frequency).

This is the index of benign publisher participation. Half the people participating in this survey, after adjustment for circulation size, gave the publishers of their papers a score of three or more out of the possible four. The distribution with the three types of respondents (publishers, editors, and staff) combined was:

Index of Benign Publisher Participation

0	1	2	3	4
8%	14%	26%	28%	23%

Other kinds of publisher intervention are not so benign. To label them as malign might seem needlessly pejorative, but it does help us to maintain a clear distinction between the two indices. And these are certainly kinds of intervention which an editor is not so likely to welcome. The indicators of malign participation are the following:

1. The publisher sometimes asks for special handling of an article about a company or organization which has some economic clout over the newspaper (any frequency).

2. The publisher sometimes asks for special handling of an article about an organization or individual with whom he has strong social ties (any frequency).

3. The publisher sometimes asks the editor to send a reporter on a non-news mission for the company: to influence legislation for example, or gather information on competition (any frequency).

4. The paper publishes editorial matter controlled by the business office on behalf of advertisers in the news columns (commonly known as "blurbs" or "business office musts") (any frequency).

As with the other index, these items are intercorrelated, meaning that a publisher perceived as doing any one of these things has a better than random chance of being seen as doing the others as well. Scoring one point for each item produces an index of malign publisher participation, and half the people in the survey (including publishers, who scored themselves) scored the publishers at two or higher.

Index of Malign Publisher Participation

0	1	2	3	4
30%	22%	23%	18%	7%

With every publisher thus measured on each of these two indices, we may now proceed to establishment of a definition of publisher types. Each publisher can be ranked as high or low on each scale, with the cutting points set to make the high and low categories of equal size. The cutting points are between 2 and 3 for the benign scale and between 1 and 2 on the malign scale.

The result is a typing system with four categories. A moment's reflection shows that the four types are indeed quite different. To keep track of them and, again, not meaning to be judgmental or disparaging, we should label these categories.

A publisher who scores low on both scales is clearly one who does not have very much to do with the news-editorial product, and so he can be labeled an "Absentee" publisher. For many in the category, that will be an overstatement, of course, but strong names do help us keep track of the categories.

The publisher who scores high on the benign scale but low on malign activity is one who confines his intervention to well-intentioned purpose and is, we surmise, beloved by editors. Call him a "Statesman."

That publisher's opposite number, the one who intervenes only for less-than-noble purposes deserves a less flattering label. "Partisan" will do.

Finally, there is the publisher who is into everything, intervening for good and bad causes alike. The net effect may be good or bad, it is hard to tell, but the label is easy: "Politician."

The following diagram makes the model easy to visualize:

PUBLISHER TYPES
Benign Participation
High   Low

		High	Low
High		Politician	Partisan
Malign Participation			
Low		Statesman	Absentee

And how are publishers distributed across these four categories? Because the two scales are not themselves correlated, a random distribution would make them about equal in size. However, when the ratings by the different kinds of persons who answered these questions are considered, they are not equal at all. The publisher type depends very much on the job of the person doing the rating. The percentages below are, of course, circulation adjusted.

Publisher Category by Rating Group

	Editors	Publishers	Staff	Consensus
Politicians	26%	28%	31%	28%
Partisans	19	10	32	20
Statesmen	19	38	13	23
Absentees	36	23	24	29

From the editor's point of view, the Absentee publisher is the most common. Publishers, however, are more likely to see themselves as Statesmen than anything else. And the ever-cynical staff sees publishers as mostly Partisans and Politicians. The purpose of this exercise is not, however, to learn how many publishers fall into each category. The division, remember, depends on cutting points set for analytical convenience. What we really want to know is how a publisher's style affects ethical positions. Before getting to that, however, it is worthwhile to consider what sort of publishers fit into each of these slots as defined by the consensus.

The most visible factor in determining a publisher's style is the size of the newspaper. Readers of small papers (under 30,000 circulation) are three times as likely to have Politician publishers—the ones who are into everything—as are readers of the larger papers (100,000 and over). At the larger papers, the Absentee publisher is the type most frequently encountered. The most desirable of the active publishers, the Statesmen, are found with about equal frequency in all of the size groupings. And the Partisans have a slight tendency to be found more often among the larger papers. The following table gives the circulation-adjusted comparisons.

Publisher Category by Newspaper Size

	Small	Medium	Large
Politician	47%	33%	14%
Partisan	15	19	23
Statesman	21	23	25
Absentee	16	25	38

The kind of ownership also makes a difference. Statesmen are found more frequently at newspapers owned by publicly held groups while Politicians and Partisans are found less frequently there. This raises an issue not often considered in the literature of journalism criticism: the effect of public ownership on newspaper companies. There has been some study of the effect of group ownership in general, and some critics have concluded that readers do not consistently benefit from the economies and opportunities which group ownership provides. Gerald L. Grotta (Journalism Quarterly, Summer, 1971), for example, found that "consumers pay higher prices under consolidated ownership with no compensating increase in quality or quantity of product received and perhaps a decrease in quality." The trend of the past 15 years toward public ownership now adds a new dimension to that kind of analysis, and it raises new questions.

As far as publisher styles are concerned, newspapers owned by privately-held groups are more like non-group papers while those owned by publicly-held companies stand apart.

Publisher Category by Ownership

	Non-Group	Private Group	Public Group
Politician	32%	33%	18%
Partisan	20	23	15
Statesman	18	19	33
Absentee	29	24	34

To the extent that Statesmen and Absentees are the most desirable kinds of publisher from the editor's point of view, newspapers owned by publicly-held groups have a clear advantage. Why do they have it? Perhaps the need to answer to shareholders fosters professionalism and editorial-side strength. Whatever the cause, the difference appears too great to be an accident.

The fact that publishers differ in their ways of relating to editors is interesting in itself. But what we really want to know is whether the publisher style has something to do with ethical outcomes. Before tackling that question, we need to take a closer look at the variety of ethical problems.

PART FOUR

The Range of Ethical Problems

Ethical issues in the newspaper business can range from the trivial to the profound. Some questions are encountered frequently and others hardly at all. In order to size up the current state of ethical concerns, we needed an objective measure that would tap both the seriousness of different kinds of problems and the frequency with which they are encountered. The study's interviewers used the initial telephone contact with editors to take a rough count of ethical problems.

It was reasoned that an ethical problem was relatively trivial if it could be solved on the spot without discussion. By "trivial," we do not mean that the consequences for those involved were necessarily unimportant, but simply that reaching a solution did not require any mental anguish. And so our objective indicator for defining a problem as nontrivial was simply that solving it require some discussion in the newsroom. A problem whose solution is so obvious that it can be reached without discussion is really no problem at all. Accordingly, editors were read a list of 12 kinds of ethical problems, and asked how frequently cases of each type were discussed at their newspapers. The list came from a survey of recent literature on newspaper ethics. The works relied on most heavily were John L. Hulteng's review of the ASNE ethical code, *Playing It Straight*, Bruce M. Swain's anecdote-rich *Reporters' Ethics*, and a work sponsored by the Hastings Center, *Teaching Ethics in Journalism Education*, by Clifford G. Christians and Catherine L. Covert.

By far the most troublesome area for newspapers—with troublesome thus defined—is the general area of fairness, balance, and objectivity, including the allocation of space to opposing interest groups or political candidates and providing the right of reply to criticism. Editors representing 64 percent of the nation's daily circulation said such problems were discussed at their newspapers at least once a month. No other class of problems came close.

This response should come as no surprise to experienced news people. An editor must mediate among a rich array of competing interests and viewpoints, and perceptions of unfairness by any of them are likely to be met with vocal objection. Ironically, the harder a newspaper tries to cover the news, the more difficult it is to satisfy the conflicting claims for attention. For a newspaper with an aggressive news staff, concerns of fairness and balance can become a continuing preoccupation.

After this primary grouping of ethical problems comes a cluster of secondary concerns which are encountered at least once a month by editors representing from a fourth to a third of total circulation. For these concerns, fairness to individuals, rather than groups, is more likely to be involved. Thirty-nine percent (circulation-adjusted) said they had discussions involving invasion of privacy—defined as news that causes injury to feelings or discloses embarrassing private facts—at least once a month.

Encountered at nearly the same rate, 36 percent, is the set of problems relating to granting and preserving confidentiality—including situations where a pledge of confidentiality involves potential harm to the reader as well as the source by withholding relevant information about that source.

Problems involving photos which might depict violence or obscenity or lead to hurt feelings are also in this secondary group, with a 29 percent rating. Then, at 26 percent, there is the whole set of problems relating to pressure from advertisers: blurbs, business office musts, keeping things out of the paper to please advertisers—or putting them in.

The problems on the list remaining proved to be relatively rare, with editors representing less than 20 percent of total circulation encountering them monthly or more often. In order of their frequency ratings, they are:

• Government secrecy: grand jury leaks, national security problems, including military secrets and diplomatic leaks— 18 percent.

• Economic temptations: accepting trips, meals, favors, loans, or gifts from sources or suppliers—15 percent.

• Suppression of news to protect the community, as in the case of factory relocations, school closings, highway expansion and the like—11 percent.

• Questionable news gathering methods, such as using false identity, stolen documents, concealed recordings, or eavesdropping—8 percent.

• Civil disorder: publicizing rioters, terrorists, bomb threats at the risk of encouraging imitators—7 percent.

• Use of reporters for non-news tasks, e.g., writing advertising supplements, gathering data for the company's financial decisions or labor relations objectives—2 percent.

The exact frequency distribution—on a scale from "never" to "several times a week" for each of the dozen classes of problems may be found in the appendix to this report.

So far in this survey of the ethical landscape, there are few surprises. But when we get down to cases, some unexpected patterns emerge. The 12-category classification scheme for ethical issues used in the interviews with editors has a certain intellectual neatness to it, but a prudent investigator will wonder whether the real world is really that neat.

If it were, attitudes toward specific ethical situations would fit into the same neatly-ordered bins. A person sensitive to one kind of fairness and balance problem would be sensitive to others, assuming that newspaper people, in reaching their real-world ethical positions, are as consistent as we who only theorize expect them to be.

To find the threads of consistency, the mail survey of editors, publishers, and staff members asked for preferred decisions on a list of hypothetical, but reality-inspired, ethical situations. By finding the clusters of consistency in these responses, we can get a better idea of how ethical problems are resolved and see how realistic our original classification scheme was. The statistical technique is complex, but the interpretation is not. Some answers will tend to predict others. For example, if an editor who leans over backward to be fair in a specific case involving balance and objectivity is likely to also do the same on others in the same general area, then it seems reasonable to conclude that there is an underlying dimension, a general concern for fairness and balance, that different news people can be measured against. But if responses to such a question prove to be linked to those of one on some different subject, then some other underlying force is at work. The trick is to find the patterns of correlation and guess at their underlying influences.

What was found is, at first glance, surprising. Questions in the same substantive areas were not always linked in the predicted fashion. There were unexpected underlying influences. Indeed, a search for those influences leads to a conclusion that newspaper ethical positions tend to be arrived at, not so much on the basis of substantive consistency as reflected in our initial questioning of editors, as on the basis of more visceral criteria. Certain situations invoke certain journalistic reflexes, and it may be these reflexes, rather than more complicated codes, explicit or implicit, which determine the ethical outcome.

The analysis of specific situations asked about in this survey produced five broad groupings, and this categorization scheme appears to be more realistic than the original one because it does contain threads of consistency.

It also reveals some inconsistencies. For example, the original questions put to editors assumed that all matters involving reporters' methods could be lumped together. In the mail survey, several specific cases involving different sorts of questionable reporting methods were asked about.

The responses were uncorrelated, i.e., a concern for questionable methods in one situation did not mean a better-than-random chance that a similar concern would be expressed in another.

Among the consistencies that were found, some were expected and some were surprising. Among the expected: news people who worry about reporters getting too close to their sources in one situation are likely to be worried in a parallel, but different situation. The two situations are linked by an underlying standard.

This standard was forthrightly expressed by the late Edwin A. Lahey, Washington Bureau chief for the Knight Newspapers in the late 1950s and 1960s before the Knight-Ridder group was formed. Lahey was beloved for his wit and compassion and knew many powerful decision makers socially. Nevertheless, he advised reporters to "pee on your source's leg at least once a week." Maintaining a distance, he believed, preserved honesty in reporting.

One of the survey questions tapping this dimension described a Washington situation paralleling the city hall case described in Part One.

Your Washington correspondent has spent years developing friend-ships with the key people now in power, and it is paying off. He knows the town well, and they are relative newcomers, so he is frequently consulted by the White House staff and the President's political operatives before key decisions are made. Should the editor:

1. Fire the Washington correspondent.

2. Move the correspondent to another city.

3. Admonish the Washington correspondent to maintain a reasonable distance from his sources.

4. Reward the Washington correspondent for developing such a good knowledge of his subject and such loyal sources.

Editors were more reluctant than either publishers or staff members to take the extreme actions of firing or transferring the correspondent. Across all three groups, those representing 11 percent of the readers would take one of those strong steps.

When the scene was shifted from Washington to city hall, however, the ethical sensitivity of all three groups increased dramatically. Editors were still more reluctant to take strong action than were publishers or staff, but the consensus for such action rose to nearly 31 percent.

Most importantly, the two items did correlate. A person favoring strong action in one case had a better-than-random chance of favoring it in the other case. In fact, they formed a cumulative index. Nearly every-one who wanted stern treatment for the Washington correspondent also wanted it for the city hall reporter. The news people in the study can therefore be divided into three categories: those who want to fire or transfer both reporters for getting too close to their sources (11 percent), those who want to fire or transfer only one of them—in nearly all cases, the city hall reporter—(19 percent), while the majority preferred mild action—or even a reward for the reporter—in both cases.

Some interesting hypotheses about newspaper ethics are supported here. One is that ethical standards are higher closer to home. Priests and psychologists have known this for some time, and we all know how some people behave at conventions. Wanderlust, suggests psychiatrist Allen Wheelis (*The Quest for Identity*, 1958), is based more on wandering for lust than lust for wandering. Most editors are somewhat insulated from the daily ethical shocks and traumas of Washington coverage. Moreover, unless it is one of the national dailies, the people involved in the story are less likely to read it, and so complaints are less likely to reach the editor's ears. The ethical price paid for an inside story at the national level is generally less visible than when that price is paid at home.

What kinds of newspaper people express the most sensitivity to the problem of closeness to sources? Conventional wisdom suggests at least one possibility. Young people might be expected to be the most sensitive to this issue. They are less likely to have strong community ties or closeness to sources themselves. Youth is generally believed to be more idealistic; young people have not yet been exposed to the world's harsh realities that justify for older persons a greater flexibility. The hypothesis is easily tested.

We shall define a person as sensitive to this issue if he or she would fire or transfer either the Washington correspondent or the city hall reporter in the two cases cited. Because the staff members are the most sensitive to this issue, we shall look at them first. If youth is a cause, then the younger staffers should be the most likely to support harsh action against a reporter for being too close to sources.

Age of Staff

	23–46	47–82	Total
Readers served by pro-action staff:	44%	6%	39%

The hypothesis has very strong support, where staff members are concerned. Among editors, age also makes a difference, although not nearly as much.

Age of Editors

	23–46	47–82	Total
Readers served by pro-action editors:	28%	18%	22%

Among publishers, age makes no difference at all:

Age of Publishers

	23–46	47–82	Total
Readers served by pro-action pubs:	33%	30%	31%

The staff members most likely to favor firing or transferring a reporter for being too cozy with sources are those who, in addition to being young, work for medium or large papers and have some post-graduate education. Neither education nor size of paper predicted this attitude among editors and publishers.

Does this mean that an elite corps of young, idealistic newspaper staff people is leading the industry toward increased sensitivity toward the need for reporter-source independence? No. It seems more likely that the staff is a conservative force resisting leadership coming from other sources and moving in another direction. Michael J. O'Neill, former editor of the New York Daily News, said in his farewell speech to the American Society of Newspaper Editors that the adversary model of reporter-source relationships has been pushed too far. His concern has been echoed by other industry leaders who sense a loss of public confidence and are reacting to it. The young hard-liners for news-source separation are arguing for keeping conventional news-gathering values. The possibility of a generation gap—with youth, not age, occupying the conservative position—keeps appearing in these data.

The next cluster of attitudes defines another traditional ethical standard in the newspaper business: that financial conflict of interest should be avoided. Financial conflict was asked about in three quite different kinds of situations, and the responses, despite this variety, were intercorrelated—meaning that a person who opposed financial conflict in one case was likely to do so in the others as well. This consistency confirms the belief with which we began that financial conflict is one of the tests by which news people evaluate conduct. The fact that it affects such diverse cases suggests that it is a very strong standard. One of the three questionnaire items was:

The business manager of the company has developed close friendships with Canadian newsprint suppliers, reinforced by regular hunting trips in the north woods as their guest. The company decides to prohibit managers from accepting favors from suppliers. The business manager continues to take the trips. Should the publisher:

1. Fire the business manager.

2. Impose discipline short of firing and extract a promise that it will not happen again.

3. Advise the business manager to pay his own way on these trips or reciprocate by hosting the suppliers on equivalent outings.

4. Decide that the no-favor rule should not apply to such long-standing and clearly benign activities.

The consensus answer was the second of the four choices, although editors representing more than a fourth of the circulation were for firing the manager. The staff, on this issue, was more tolerant than either the editors or the publishers.

A second item in the series dealt with staff malfeasance:

The chief photographer moonlights as a wedding photographer. The father of a bride calls the editor and says the photographer has made a sales pitch to his daughter and included a sly hint that if he is hired for the job, her picture has a better chance of making the society page. The editor investigates and confirms that this is the photographer's regular practice. Should the editor:

1. Fire the photographer.

2. Impose lesser discipline and order the photographer to stop moonlighting.

3. Allow the photographer to continue moonlighting, but order him not to use—or pretend to use—his position to gain favored treatment for clients.

4. Ask the photographer to be more discreet.

Close to half said they would fire the photographer. Editors, publishers and staff were in close agreement.

The third item was discussed in Section One. It deals with the reporter who develops information which would affect his own finances adversely and decides to suppress it. Editors took a much harder line than staff members.

These three items can be combined into an index which measures sensitivity to financial conflict of interest. The procedure in this case was to award one point for the extreme action in each case. Any value judgment as to whether such actions were right or wrong may be postponed for the moment. The extreme actions were (1) insisting that the reporter leave the financially damaging information in the story, (2) firing the moonlighting photographer, and (3) firing the junketing business manager. The distribution across all three groups was:

Sensitivity to Financial Conflict of Interest

	0	1	2	3
Publishers	22%	41%	25%	13%
Editors	16	38	27	19
Staff	22	38	31	8
Everyone	20	39	28	13

For the purpose of crosstabulation—which works best if the categories are of nearly equal size—the survey participants were classified as high on this measure if they asked for the extreme measure in at least two out of the three cases.

Who are the news people who are most sensitive to financial conflict?

They are overwhelmingly young, and, this time, the age difference was visible in all three groups, most clearly where publishers were concerned. Nearly half of the youngest group of publishers (circulation-adjusted), but less than 30 percent of the oldest group ranked as highly sensitive on this issue. The oldest editors were less sensitive than younger ones, and the youngest staffers were twice as likely to be in the highly-sensitive group as older ones.

Staff members and editors were more sensitive on this issue if they came from large papers, and all three groups indicated greater sensitivity if their papers were owned by publicly-held corporations—yet another hint of a new variable that may affect the formation of ethical standards. There was also a suggestion of regional difference, with greater sensitivity in the east than in the west. Finally, editors were somewhat less likely to be in the high-sensitivity group if they had a high level of civic activity.

Here, as with the index on closeness to sources, we have wide support for traditional values, with young newspaper people the least compromising. As newspaper people grow older, gain in responsibility, come in increasing contact with the community, they appear to take less of a hard line on financial conflict of interest.

These two dimensions of newspaper ethics describe standards whose application is a close fit to conventional wisdom about how news people think. The third one to be examined here does not fit the established framework quite as easily.

This dimension involves what at first glance seem like three separate ethical issues: invasion of privacy, harrassment of innocent sources, and protection of government secrets. Yet, their responses are clustered. Knowing how a news person responds to one issue gives a measurable advantage in guessing where he or she will come down on the other two. An underlying thread connects them.

One of these indicators involves the publication of embarrassing

private facts: the case of the hometown homosexual who is in a resort hotel fire, which was described in Part One. The four alternatives were:
1. *Publish the story in full.*
2. *Publish the story, but without mentioning the gay angle.*
3. *Publish the story, but without mentioning the local citizen.*
4. *Kill the story.*

Publishers, editors, and staff members alike were closely divided between the first two alternatives, with a modest consensus for the second. There was only scattered support for the third alternative and virtually none for the fourth.

The next deals with harrassment of innocent but newsworthy persons:

The first refugees from the Falkland Islands come to stay with relatives in your town. You know from the Iranian hostage experience that they are likely to be harrassed and intimidated by competing news people striving for the last detail. Already, reporters and camera persons are setting up camp in the front yard. Should the editor:

1. Organize pool coverage to reduce the burden on the family.

2. Make a public plea for all media to use restraint.

3. Avoid public pronouncements, but order his own staff to use restraint.

4. Do nothing, on the theory that competitive news coverage is best for society in the long run.

The consensus response was the third, although staff members were far more willing than either editors or publishers to do nothing and enjoy the benefits of competitive news coverage. This was the second most popular course overall, with only scattered support for the first two alternatives.

The third item in the series deals with the frequently encountered problem of what to do with a grand jury leak:

Under which of the following circumstances should a newspaper publish material from leaked grand jury transcripts:

1. Whenever the material is newsworthy.

2. Whenever the importance of the material revealed outweighs the damage to the system from the breaching of its security.

3. Only if the material exposes flaws in the workings of the grand jury system itself, e.g., it shows the prosecutor to be acting improperly.

4. Never.

The second response is the most frequent in all three groups, although staff members are far more likely than editors or publishers to let newsworthiness be the only consideration.

Now the nature of the unifying thread begins to appear. Each of these items measures an underlying tendency to want to publish, regardless of the cost. We saw in Part Two how staff people prefer to err on the side of publishing more often than do their editors or publishers. Now it becomes clear that many different kinds of problems, among all three groups, are resolved on this level. The consistency suggests that the news person's urge to get the story into print can override a great variety of other considerations. Where the urge is strong—and it usually is—it can keep problems from being considered on an ethical plane at all. The decision rule that publishing is better than not publishing is simple, easy to apply, and can become almost a reflex, like a knee jerk.

As in all the other issues examined in this study, newspaper people vary. Some are possessed more than others of this urge to forge into print regardless of cost. And, as with many of the issues, it is not easy to say that one position or the other is the more ethical. There is virtue in publishing, and sometimes there is virtue in not publishing. The point here is that if an issue is resolved on the basis of an inner urge to publish or refrain from publishing, its ethical content may never reach the agenda.

To find out what kinds of news people tend to decide things one way or the other, a scale was created to measure this tendency toward self-restraint in publishing—again, without any value judgment as to whether such a tendency is good or bad. We know that it exists, and we want to know who has it.

In each of the questions just described, two of the four alternatives define somewhat greater restraint than the majority is willing to accept. By awarding each person in the survey one point for such a restraining answer, we get the following distribution:

Restraint-in-Publication Index

	0	1	2	3
Publishers	60%	30%	9%	1%
Editors	67	27	6	0
Staff	62	28	9	1
Everyone	63	28	8	1

A high-restraint group can be defined then, as composed of those news people who chose a restraining answer for at least one of the three problems in the index. Now we can use crosstabulation to see what the restraint-prone group is like.

Once again, age makes a difference, but the tension between the rigidity of young idealists and the flexibility of older people in authority is absent, or at least muddled. Among staff members, age is not a factor. Among publishers, it is, with the older publishers more ready for restraint.

A theory to explain that is easy to come by: as a person in authority grows older, he or she grows weary of the opprobrium and complaint that results from a publish-at-any-cost policy, and is more likely to think twice when publishing is questionable. If that theory is true, one might assume that it ought to apply to editors as well. But it doesn't. The younger the editor, the more restraint he or she is likely to show.

Perhaps the generation gap works differently for editors than it does for publishers. Or perhaps something else is afoot. And a probable explanation does indeed arise when we see what other factors incline an editor toward self-restraint in publication. The restraint-prone editor is likely to be at a smaller paper, in a non-competitive town. In smaller towns, the psychological costs of publication are much higher. The editor is more likely to be acquainted with the traveling homosexual, the grand jury members, and the family hosting the refugees. The pain he inflicts is very visible, and it is more difficult to think in terms of abstract principle. This size effect is most pronounced for editors, but it works for publishers and staff members as well. The following table shows the probability of a reader being served by a restraint-inclined news person at small, medium, and large newspapers.

Readers Served by Restraint-Inclined News People

	Small Papers	Medium Papers	Large Papers
Editors	51%	40%	19%
Publishers	54	51	27
Staff	56	32	32
Everybody	53	41	26

The reader of a paper with less than 30,000 daily circulation is more than twice as likely to have a restraint-leaning editor as the reader of a paper with more than 100,000 circulation. Because smaller newspapers tend to have younger editors, we cannot be sure which factor—age of the editor or size of the paper—has the most effect on self-restraint without further checking. It is a simple check: just hold newspaper size constant. We do it by making our comparisons among newspapers of a given size. When that is done, we find that age's cautioning effect disappears for small and medium size papers. For those papers, therefore, it is the small size and not the age of the editor that induces restraint. On larger papers, however, the age effect persists. For readers of papers with more than 100,000 circulation, a young (under 47) editor is twice as likely to be high on restraint as an older editor. Perhaps big-city editors are toughened more by scar tissue as they age.

Restraint is less likely in competitive markets, where the probability of being embarrassed by a decision not to publish is greater. And, for editors and staff members, there is yet another factor at work. Restraint is more likely when there is a high level of personal involvement in civic activity. Civic activity was measured in this study by the number of local voluntary organizations a news person belonged to, such as churches, civic clubs, charitable organizations, veterans groups. and the like. The averages were seven for publishers, two for editors, and one for staff members. A person was classified as having high civic involvement when his or her group's average was exceeded.

At the 1982 ASNE meeting in Chicago, Judee and Michael Burgoon spoke of the insularity of many news people and noted that those with few community contacts were more satisfied with their newspaper's professional standards. Depending on how optimistic you are, these data can be interpreted in one of two ways. Perhaps civic involvement is a corrupting influence, leading news people to depart from their deeply-held conviction that publication is almost always better than keeping secrets. On the other hand, civic involvement may sensitize news people to the consequences of what they do and make them more willing to consider restraint. Whether this sensitivity can be classed as corruption depends, of course, on how far it takes one down the road of restraint. It is precisely at this point, when a balance is being weighed, that the question becomes an ethical one. The knee-jerk response to publish at all costs may not always, nor even often, lead to bad outcomes, but it does prevent the question from ever rising to the level of an ethical issue.

Renewing our search for threads of continuity in the treatment of ethical issues by our sample of news people, we find another theme in the data which fits no substantive ethical category but seems to illuminate yet another kind of reflexive response. We caught a glimpse of it in Part One where we discovered that editors and publishers tend to divide on questions involving money—no matter what the non-financial subject matter happened to be. In probing for patterns of correlation, we now find that several money-related items tend to hang together. We shall first consider them one at a time, starting with the problem of checkbook journalism:

An investigative reporter discovers a former city employee now living in another state who has evidence of a kickback scheme involving the mayor and half the city council. He appears interested in cooperating with your investigation, but indicates that he will want money. Should your paper:

1. Pay an honorarium based on the news value of the story.
2. Put him on the payroll for the time that he spends working with your staff in gathering and documenting the facts, plus expenses.
3. Pay his out-of-pocket expenses only.
4. Pay nothing.

The consensus answer was to pay nothing, with publishers somewhat more willing than editors or staff members to break out the checkbook. A sizeable minority, representing about a third of total circulation, would reimburse for out-of-pocket expenses.

By now, the persistent reader will realize that we are going to create another index. We shall call it the anti-money index and award one point for each extreme answer in the direction of shunning money and its works. In the above case, the point is awarded for the fourth response, "pay nothing."

That response is correlated with the extreme response to the next question:

The company that owns a major metropolitan newspaper also owns a major sports franchise in that town. Should the paper:
1. Try to build up local interest in the team it owns, because it is good for community spirit as well as profitable to the company.
2. Treat the team exactly as it treats any other team.
3. Bend over backwards to be fair and treat the company-owned team with more skepticism and outright criticism than are accorded other teams.
4. Sell the franchise.

Most participants in the survey, by far, would treat the team like any other. The weak second choice, especially among staff members, was to sell the franchise.

At first glance, the next item in this series appears to be totally unrelated. But think about it:

A business writer discovers that TV sets with built-in videotex decoders will be on the local market within 60 days, greatly increasing convenience and reducing costs for people who sign up for the local videotex service—which, incidentally, is not owned by your paper. The advertising manager calls the publisher and says local TV dealers are afraid they will be stuck with an oversupply of obsolete TV sets if the word gets out. Should the publisher:
1. Order the story killed.

2. Explain the problem to the editor with a recommendation that the story be delayed.
3. Suggest to the editor that the story be double checked for accuracy.
4. Help the ad manager pacify the retailers, but say nothing to the editor.

At issue here, of course, is whether the editor should be bothered about this problem at all. There was virtually no interest in the first two choices. Publishers split about evenly (circulation adjusted) between options three and four, while editors and staff members preferred the latter by about two to one, and it is this last response that fits with those which we have called "anti-money."

The final item in the series is the Florida casino question examined previously. The anti-money response, of course, is that no newspaper should ever make a cash contribution to influence a referendum.

What ties this diverse array of subjects together? Why should a person who opposes paying money to sources also be likely to want the paper to sell its sports franchise, avoid political contributions, and not bother the editor about the problems of retailers? Calling it an anti-money bias may be too facile. What we have here may be an outcropping of the historic antipathy between the news side and the business office. Paying sources, unless it is done routinely, may call for going outside the newsroom budget and introduce the risk of business office influence. Or perhaps the response is not even made with that or any sort of rationalization. Perhaps using money to get news is too much like what the business office does and violates some barrier that may not be very clear at the conscious level.

If we define the underlying trait as business office aversion, the inclusion of the third item makes more intuitive sense. That the editor should not be bothered about advertisers' problems is an ancient, although not always strictly followed, component of traditional newsroom codes. But why should it rub off on such seemingly unrelated matters as a newspaper-owned sports franchise or the casino problem? "Rubbing off" may be exactly what is going on. The fear of abuse of economic power, based on much relevant history, may have conditioned news people to reject any unconventional use of that power. If this is the underlying trait, the problem of knee-jerk responses to ethical issues arises in a new and different form. The knee jerk may lead to the ethical answer more often than not. The problem is that it decides the issue before more careful weighing and analyzing can take place.

One need not share that fear to be interested in knowing more about the kinds of people who make the business-aversive response. To learn more about them, we must first define them. Giving one point for the extreme response in each of the four cases produces the following distribution on the index:

Index of Business Office Aversion

	0	1	2	3	4
Publishers	22%	27%	28%	21%	2%
Editors	5	30	38	23	4
Staff	9	24	34	24	9
Everybody	11	27	34	23	5

Because, for analytical convenience, we like categories to be as equally sized as possible, we shall cut this one so that anyone who gave the business-aversive answer on at least two of the four items is ranked high on this characteristic. That means 61 percent will be high, and now we can see who they are by looking at the crosstabulations.

The most consistent predictor of business-side aversion is low civic involvement. It works for publishers, editors and staff alike.

Readers Served by Business-Side Aversive News People

	Low Civic Activity	High Civic Activity
Publishers	64%	34%
Editors	71	52
Staff	73	58
Everybody	70	47

To be specific, the reader of a paper whose publisher is low in civic activity has a 64 percent chance of having that publisher be business-side aversive as we have defined it. But a reader whose publisher is high in civic activity has only a 34 percent chance of finding that publisher in the business-aversive group.

Circulation size also makes some difference. Staff members of large papers are more business-aversive. For editors, the difference is more modest. And for publishers, size makes no difference at all.

Readers Served by Business-Side Aversive News People

	Small	Medium	Large
Publishers	53%	51%	50%
Editors	55	68	68
Staff	53	63	78
Everybody	54	61	66

Note that as circulation size increases, the differences among publishers, editors, and staff increase. At the smaller papers, those under 30,000, there is very close agreement.

Age also has some effect, with younger people more likely to be high on the business-aversive index. And there is a hint of a regional difference, with the high people on the scale found less frequently in the South.

What these characteristics seem to point to is insularity. The aversives are young, city people, with low civic involvement. But there is another way to look at it. If business office aversion is considered basically good—and newspaper tradition holds that it is—then the civic ties which represent the cure for insularity are rightly viewed as corrupting. Publishers, editors, and staff members are all closer to the business office and to the advertisers in a small place than in a large city and perhaps freer to decide questions such as those which form the index on their merits rather than on rigid rules of separation. Or they may be less free to act with the independence which the codes demand. What does seem certain is that a person's ties to the community have a lot to do with ethical outcomes, but it is not at all clear whether those ties tend to produce good outcomes or bad. And to the extent that these influences suggest reflexive rather than rational approaches to ethical problems, news people may not be meeting their responsibilities to the public as effectively as they might.

It has become increasingly clear that the groupings of ethical problems arrived at in this way differ from the traditional categories which were assumed at the start of this study. The final index to be considered, however, has more of a traditional look. It is composed of three items whose common thread appears to be a desire to give even-handed treatment to groups and individuals in the news. In short, it measures some aspect of fairness, balance, and objectivity. It is not a comprehensive measure because many items involving fairness do not correlate with it. But it is tapping something real, and it is related to the broader category which, as we discovered at the beginning of this chapter, is the traditional category which editors found usually causes more newsroom discussion than any other.

Three items fit clearly in this list, and the first deals with the sensibilities of religious minorities.

Easter Sunday is approaching, and the editor plans the traditional page-one recognition of the holiday: A banner, "He is Risen." Then a new publisher, who happens to be an agnostic, points out that the latest religious census shows the community to be six percent non-Christian. Should the editor:

1. Keep the Easter banner.

2. Reduce the size of the headline in deference to the non-Christians in the community.
3. Limit the paper's coverage to specific religious-oriented events scheduled for that day.
4. Avoid any mention of Easter.

Participants in the survey were sharply polarized between the first and third choices, with only scattered support for the others. Publishers were for keeping the Easter banner by two-to-one, while editors were about evenly divided, and a slight majority of staff members would limit Easter coverage to specific events rather than keep the banner. In forming the index, a choice of either of the latter two alternatives was interpreted as indicating a strong tendency toward fairness and balance. Those who wanted to preserve some observance of Easter in the newspaper were asked how large the non-Christian segment of the community should become before they would modify their response. The average was close to 50 percent across all three groups.

Sensitivity to this issue was associated with concern for fairness in a very different kind of case not involving religion at all:

A local boy who grew up in poverty makes good by educating himself, working hard, and becoming a successful businessman. This effort culminates in opening of the fanciest restaurant the town has yet seen. His younger brother has also made good, in a way, by becoming an editorial writer, and he salutes his brother's Horatio Alger story in a folksy and appealing signed column. To ward off any charge of conflict of interest, he identifies himself as the brother of the subject of the piece in the opening paragraph. Should the editor:
1. Kill the column.
2. Have the column rewritten to eliminate the brother's name and the name of the restaurant.
3. Move the piece to some less conspicuous part of the paper.
4. Let it stand.

The consensus, by a large margin, was to let the column stand, with little disagreement among editors, publishers, and staff members. But news people representing about a fourth of total readership thought the piece should either be killed or rewritten to eliminate mention of the brother's name and the restaurant. These two responses were used to denote strong sensitivity to fairness. Whether they represent excessive sensitivity is not, of course, an issue to be addressed here—at least not just yet.

The third item in the fairness category presents an issue that is totally different from the first two—and yet response from those two tend to predict response to this one, suggesting that all three are tapping the same underlying attitude. This one can be interpreted as involving fairness to the readers or fairness to the competition, at the cost of some journalistic pride. The situation still occurs, despite decreasing competition among local daily newspapers. It sometimes happens when the national media are pursuing the same story, or it happens when newspapers and broadcast media are on the same hot trail. Just how does one deal with the competition when it becomes part of the news?

A scandal is unfolding in city government, and your paper is getting more than its share of the news beats. But, today, your paper is beaten by a competing medium on a key element of the story. Should your paper:
1. Treat the new element just as though the competition had never mentioned it.
2. Acknowledge the competition's beat in print and cover the story according to its intrinsic news value.
3. Downgrade the importance of the new element.
4. Ignore the new element.

Most news people with experience in competitive situations can provide at least anecdotal evidence that downgrading or ignoring a story that the opposition got first is not uncommon. But no one, apparently, approves of such a practice. Survey participants were virtually unanimous in support of the first two options. Publicly acknowledging the competition's beat in print was the consensus choice, by news people representing 59 percent of readers. Publishers, editors, and staff members were in close agreement. This choice was used to indicate sensitivity to fairness in constructing the index.

We have, therefore, an index in which respondents had three opportunities to give an answer indicating a high degree of concern for fairness. Here's how their responses were distributed.

Index of Fairness, Balance, and Objectivity

	0	1	2	3
Publishers	30%	37%	19%	14%
Editors	22	37	31	10
Staff	20	36	34	11
Everybody	24	36	28	12

Publishers are somewhat more likely than editors or staff to score a zero on this index, but the differences are not great. For crosstabbing, anyone with a score of two or three (the top 40 percent in terms of readers) was considered highly sensitive to fairness issues. Who are they?

Religion has an effect on this index, the result, no doubt, of the religious content of one of the questions. Jews in all three categories, editors, publishers, and staffers, were more likely than members of other faiths to score high. So were people in all three groups who do not attend religious services frequently.

People working on large papers were more likely to register high scores for fairness and balance than those on smaller papers. For editors, the difference was especially great:

Readers Represented by News People High on Fairness and Balance

	Small	Medium	Large
		Newspaper Size	
Publishers	21%	25%	43%
Editors	22	25	61
Staff	31	49	49
Everybody	25	33	51

Those in competitive markets and those whose papers are owned by publicly-held companies are also more likely to score high on the fairness-and-balance index. For publishers and staff members, those who are young and relatively low in civic activity are higher in sensitivity to issues of fairness and balance. For editors, neither factor makes much difference.

Publishers are far more likely to score high on fairness and balance if they have previously worked on the news-editorial side. And the longer their time of such service, the greater the probability of being sensitive to these issues. For readers whose publishers had previous news-side experience, the probability that their publishers would rank high on fairness and balance was nearly double. The difference was 39 percent to 20 percent. When publishers had more than 22 years of news background behind them, the rate of fairness-and-balance sensitivity rose to 50 percent.

Perhaps we now have enough data to venture a broad conclusion or two. News people, in the formation and execution of ethical standards, are subject to two opposing forces, one external and one internal. The internal force consists of the body of journalistic lore, tradition, almost a tribal memory, whose primary values are honesty and independence. It provides the proverbial touch of starch in the backbone of the young reporter who goes out to question the high and the mighty. It places accuracy at the top of the list of objectives and demands that the journalist stand far enough apart from what he observes so that his view remains untainted by special interest or subjective judgment. The inner-directed journalist, like the inner-directed forebear of modern man cited by David Riesman, Reuel Denny and Nathan Glazer (*The Lonely Crowd*, 1950) learns these standards so thoroughly that he or she can act on them instantly and intuitively without conscious analytical effort. The standards are learned from role models in the newsroom, from journalism teachers, and even from textbooks. If there is rigidity in the standards and their application, it is at least partly because the daily pressures and temptations for relaxing the standards are so great that only a rigid and automatic response can deal with them efficiently.

The external force comes from the community which the newspaper serves. This community has standards and values of its own, and it is interested more in substantive outcomes than in processes. Cooperation for civic betterment is high on its list of objectives, and it expects the newspaper to be part of the cooperative effort and not a perpetual or reflexive antagonist. These civic values clash with journalistic values, not when journalists behave unethically by traditional standards of the profession, but when the traditional standards are applied rigidly and unthinkingly.

These standards, as examination of the five indices has shown, tend to be observed most consistently by young news people who work for large papers and whose civic activity is low. Those who are older, who work for smaller papers, and who have high involvement in civic activity, are more flexible.

If this conflict between inner and other-directed ethical systems indeed defines the problem, is there a solution? Can the rigid application of traditional journalistic standards be relaxed without inviting the very evils they were formed to ward off? Can a new ethic, which calls for more thoughtful analysis of individual cases and fewer knee-jerk responses be formed? Is it needed?

Many news people believe that current problems could be bypassed if only the public understood the underlying need for journalists to behave the way they do. Indeed, it is a majority view. Two-thirds of the reading public is served by news people who agree with the statement, "Public concern over newspaper ethics is caused less by the things newspapers do than by their failure to explain what they do." Taken literally, this view holds that newspaper ethics is more of a problem of public relations than one of substance, and it denotes a certain smugness. Who is likely to hold this view—the young, big-city, inner-directed news people or the older, less insular people? The answer is not completely clear, but the latter group appears to have the edge on smugness. Newspaper size was a consistent predictor among editors, publishers, and staff.

Readers Served by News People Who View Ethics As a PR Problem
Newspaper Size

	Small	Medium	Large
Publishers	75%	73%	62%
Editors	81	69	69
Staff	64	62	56
Everybody	73	68	63

Age made a difference for publishers, but not for staff members. The older, more experienced publishers were more likely to hold that explaining newspaper behavior was more important than changing it. Civic involvement was also a strong predictor of this attitude, with newspaper people who are high in civic activity the most likely to see ethics as a communication problem.

Positions on substantive ethical issues have very little to do with this attitude, with one exception. News people who are more ready than others to favor self-restraint in publishing are more likely to hold the ethics-as-PR view. This profile lends itself to an encouraging interpretation. Those news people who are most likely to ride the traditional ethic to an adversarial extreme are also the least comfortable with the current behavior of their newspapers. They are at least more likely to believe that the industry's ethical problems are real ones and not just a matter of being misunderstood. The potential for self-criticism and thoughtful evaluation appears to exist where it is most needed.

PART FIVE

Publisher Styles and Ethical Values

Earlier in this report, we examined four basic types of publishers according to their operating styles:

- The Statesman, whose editorial-side activity is confined to helping make improvements to the paper.
- The Partisan, who intervenes only to obtain favored treatment for friends or advertisers.
- The Politician, who intervenes for both purposes.
- The Absentee, who does not intervene at all.

We would expect these different types of publishers to hold somewhat different ethical values, and now we are in a position to see if this is so. Five indices measuring different ethical dimensions have been defined, and we can see how the different publisher types rank on each of them.

For this comparison, we shall assign each publisher to one of the four categories according to the editor's evaluation of the publisher's behavior. Publishers' self-evaluations may be unduly kind, while the staff ratings are likely to be unduly cynical. The editor enjoys the closest working relationship with the publisher and he or she has the information needed for our definitions. Therefore, the tables to follow will examine publisher's self-expressed ethical values broken down by their operating styles as seen by their editors.

If our publisher classification scheme is to work as we expect, we should find that the Statesman, the publisher who eschews interference to obtain favored treatment for individuals or groups, but who does interfere to improve the editorial product, will show the greatest sensitivity to ethical concerns. And that is what we do find in at least one case, the index of sensitivity to fairness, balance, and objectivity. However, it could be wrong to conclude that the Statesman's exposure to newsroom concerns is the source of this sensitivity, because the Absentee, the publisher who stays out of the newsroom altogether, is nearly as sensitive. Moreover, this greater sensitivity on the part of the Statesman is not consistent across all classifications of ethical problems. Here's how the four publisher types stack up on the fairness-and-balance index. This table compares the percentage of readers with publishers who rank high on the index.

	Politician	Statesman	Partisan	Absentee
Sensitive to Fairness and Balance:	23%	40%	24%	37%

This table is reassuring because of all the clusters of ethical values found in this survey, fairness and balance is perhaps the closest match to traditional and generally accepted newsroom values. However, concern for financial conflict is just as traditional, and here we find the Politician ranking high while the Statesman is low. Only the Absentee is consistent with another high rating.

	Politician	Statesman	Partisan	Absentee
Sensitive to Financial conflict:	42%	29%	24%	45%

Why should publishers who are highly active on the news side and the publishers who are not active at all score higher than those with limited activity? Before trying to arrive at a simple theory to explain everything—which may or may not be possible—let us look at the other indices.

On the issue of closeness to sources, we find that Statesmen and Absentees are the most sensitive:

	Politician	Statesman	Partisan	Absentee
Sensitive to Closeness to sources:	25%	38%	24%	31%

The remaining indices show hardly any differences among the publisher types. When business-office aversion is measured, we might expect the Partisan to score lower than the others, and he does, although the difference is not great.

	Politician	Statesman	Partisan	Absentee
Business aversion:	52%	56%	44%	56%

When the issue is self-restraint in publication, the four groups are again about the same except for the Absentee, who evidences a stronger bias in favor of publishing. The percentages in this table are indicating readers whose publishers show a high degree of self-restraint.

	Politician	Statesman	Partisan	Absentee
High in restraint:	48%	46%	48%	31%

A full explanation for this pattern of differences in values must await further investigation, but pieces of it can be seen to make some sense. The Absentee publisher scores the most consistently according to traditional values, and it may be because his absence from the newsroom shelters him from any challenges to those traditional values. If the Politician is low in traditional values, it may not be due so much to a lack of concern for ethical problems as for a tendency to appreciate the subtleties of those problems gained from everyday contact with them and a habit of evaluating them on a case-by-case basis. It is important to remember that as these indices are constructed, the high score is not necessarily the most ethical score. A high scorer might be someone whose knee-jerk reactions or hypersensitivity to ethical problems removes him as far from logical and thoughtful consideration of the problems as someone at the opposite end of the scale who is totally insensitive. High scores, as we have seen in the previous chapter, may demonstrate a readiness to push traditional newsroom standards to an adversarial extreme. An Absentee publisher, these data suggest, is more ready than others to tolerate such an outcome.

Viewed in this light, a certain amount of inconsistency might be socially and professionally desirable. Less consistent responses could mean that the codes, to the extent they exist, are not being blindly and thoughtlessly applied.

If this hypothesis has merit, if it is true that newsroom involvement makes codes seem less practical, then the Politicians among the publishers in our sample should be the least inclined to favor formal ethical codes and the Absentee should be the most committed to code ethics. Fortunately, the survey was able to measure this. The question was asked in several different ways, including the following:

Some newspaper people believe that every newspaper should have a written code of ethics or set of guidelines that its staff could consult when ethical problems came up. Others say that every situation is different, and each ethical problem needs to be considered on its own merits. Which comes closest to your belief?

The hypothesis works. Absentees are significantly more likely than Politicians to be code ethicists. The breakdown (in terms of readers):

	Politicians	Statesmen	Partisans	Absentees
Support for code ethics:	40%	56%	69%	73%

The pattern persists when the question is put more generally:

These are two statements about ethics. Please tell me which one of them comes closest to your view:
   1. In deciding ethical questions, one should refer to certain universal truths about right and wrong which never change.
   2. There are few, if any, universal truths, and each question should be decided according to what benefits the community in the long run.

Again, readers with Absentee publishers were far more likely to have publishers who favor code ethics (the first choice, above) over situation ethics than were readers with Politicians for publishers. The distribution:

	Politicians	Statesmen	Partisans	Absentees
Code ethics:	62%	60%	65%	83%

It therefore appears that the idea of codifying ethical principles, while popular overall, is most accepted among publishers who are least likely to get their hands dirty with real-life application of those codes.

The connection we have just made is more profound than it may appear at first glance. We have found a link between an attitude (what the publisher thinks of code ethics) and a behavior (publisher's management style). This linkage is especially credible because the two measurements come from different sources. We have the publisher's self-report on code ethics and the editor's report on that publisher's management style. Too often in attitude research, what appears to be a connection between attitude and behavior turns out to be two redundant statements of the same attitude. A person's self-report of a behavior may be colored by the attitude with which it is correlated. By getting an external measure of the behavior, we have avoided that problem. We have also shown that there is substance behind our classification of publisher types.

This should bestir us to look for other effects (or perhaps causes) of publisher style. One variable that should interest us is newsroom morale. Generally, an organization which is unified, goal-directed, and shares common aims and values will be a happier unit than one which is at odds with itself, uncertain, and lacking in leadership. What kind of publishing style yields the happiest newsroom? If the traditional model of separation of business and editorial functions is the most efficient, the paper with an Absentee for publisher should be happiest. Its newsroom is free to pursue news-side values untainted by the profit motive and led by an editor who is left alone by the publisher. That, at least, is what newsroom folklore tells us.

What we find, however, is just the reverse. The newsroom of a paper with an Absentee for a publisher, is among the least happy. The happiest newsroom is found at the paper whose publisher takes an active role in producing and enhancing the editorial product—the Statesman. Here is the distribution where morale in the newsroom is estimated by the publishers themselves. They used a scale of one to ten and in this breakdown a happy newsroom is defined as one rated at eight or better.

	Politicians	Statesmen	Partisans	Absentees
Readers served by happy newsrooms:	46%	58%	40%	30%

Here again, the two related phenomena are being measured by different observers. It is the editor who provides the data by which we classify the publishers, and it is the publisher who estimates newsroom morale. But is the publisher the best judge of morale in the newsroom? For a check, let us see how the same table looks when the editor is the judge of morale.

	Politicians	Statesmen	Partisans	Absentees
Happy newsrooms (Editor evaluation):	36%	54%	37%	37%

The Statesman has the highest newsroom morale, regardless of whether it is the editor or the publisher making the judgment.

Another measure of the relative efficiency of different publisher styles is possible. In an ethically efficient operation, the editor and the publisher should respect one another's judgment and ability to deal with ethical matters. If they are hostile or suspicious of one another, the chances are increased that they are working at cross purposes with unpredictable results.

The survey asked editors and publishers to rate one another. The question was phrased like this: "On a scale of A to F—with A being the highest grade and F being a failing grade, how would you rate the ability of your publisher (editor) to deal with ethical matters?"

Here's how the different kinds of publishers view their editors. The numbers are the percent in each publisher category (adjusted for circulation) who give their editors an "A."

	Politicians	Statesmen	Partisans	Absentees
A-rated editors:	53%	80%	46%	71%

Statesmen have the highest regard for their editors, but Absentees are close behind. Partisans and Politicians have the least respect for their editors.

These feelings were reciprocated only in part. Editors like Statesmen the most and Absentees second. But the regard which Politicians profess for their editors is not returned in kind at all. Even the lowly Partisan —who intervenes for selfish purposes—is better regarded by editors than is the Politician. Here is the distribution:

	Politicians	Statesmen	Partisans	Absentees
A-rated publishers:	20%	72%	34%	61%

Surprisingly, editors' evaluation of their publishers were, for the most part, independent of publishers views on substantive ethical issues. The most visible exception was publisher standing on the issue of a reporter's closeness to sources. This characteristic, you will recall, was measured by a stated willingness to take strong action to discourage a Washington reporter or a city hall reporter from getting too friendly with sources. Publishers who take the hard line on traditional separation of reporters and sources are significantly more likely to be respected by their editors. The circulation-adjusted breakdown:

Publisher Support for Separation of Reporters and Sources		
	Weak	Strong
A-rated publishers:	36%	64%

For the other ethical clusters, the publisher's belief had little or nothing to do with what the editor thought of him. The editor's evaluation depended more on procedural or background variables—age, for example. Older publishers got higher marks:

Age of Publisher		
23-46	47-55	56-82
40%	46%	53%

(A-rated publishers:)

Editors evidently like direction even if they don't like a publisher's visible presence so much. The highest-rated publishers were those whose papers had formal written codes of ethics. But the rating was even higher if the publisher admitted that he didn't know where to put his hands on that code right at the moment.

Conventional wisdom holds that editors prefer publishers who have been on the editorial side themselves, and this would lead us to expect that those publishers with news-side experience get higher ethical marks from their editors than those without. It was not so, however. In fact, there was a slight difference in the other direction with the publishers who do not have such experience somewhat more likely to get the better evaluations from editors.

Other factors contributing to a high rating for publishers: education beyond the bachelor's degree; a large, competitive market; residence in the area of publication; and, to a modest degree, presence of an ombudsman column in the newspaper.

Finally, a basic psychological characteristic made a difference. Everyone in the survey was asked two questions which measure a general trust in other people. They are based on a scale first developed by Morris Rosenberg in the 1950s and later modified by the Survey Research Center at the University of Michigan. They ask:

Do you think most people would try to take advantage of you if they got a chance, or would they try to be fair?

Generally speaking, would you say that most people can be trusted or that you can't be too careful in dealing with most people?

Publishers who gave the cynical answer to either question were far less likely to be well-regarded by their editors for ethical abilities. A reader with such a cynical publisher has only a 24 percent chance of having that publisher judged ethically able by his editor. A reader with a trusting publisher has more than double the chance: 49 percent.

When publishers rate their editors on ability to deal with ethical concerns, the pattern is quite different. The substantive positions of the editors have a great deal to do with how those editors are rated by their publishers. For each of the five dimensions used in this study, editors who give the traditional responses get the highest marks. It is true even for business-office aversion, with the aversive editors considered by their publishers to be more ethically able. The effect is stronger with some scales than others. and the two scales with the most direct measures of traditional values—for fairness, balance, and objectivity and against financial conflict of interest—showing the strongest relationship.

	Sensitivity to Financial Conflict	
	Low	High
A-rated editors:	56%	75%

	Sensitivity to Fairness and Balance	
	Low	High
A-rated editors:	57%	78%

The editor who expresses the traditional bias in favor of publishing in cases where there is some doubt is also more likely to be well-regarded by the publisher than one who shows some self-restraint. The difference here was modest, however. A reader whose editor is low in self-restraint has a 68 percent chance of having that editor rated "A" in ethical ability by the publisher. For the high-self-restraint editor, the probability is 56 percent.

Editors of large papers got better marks than those of small papers. If the paper is owned by a company whose stock is publicly traded, the editor's rating goes up sharply. The reader of such a paper has a 75 percent chance of drawing a well-regarded editor, as opposed to only 58 percent for the reader of a paper that is part of a privately-held group or not in any group at all. While not conclusive, this suggests, particularly when considered with findings mentioned earlier, that the need to make public accounting to shareholders promotes professionalism at many newspapers.

We saw earlier that editors were kinder in their judgments of publishers when their publishers were older. When publishers judge editors, the age bias is reversed, with publishers giving their better ratings to editors who are somewhat younger and less experienced than editors as a whole. Editors who are below the norm in level of civic activity are also more likely to get good marks for ethical ability. Finally, an ombudsman column helps the editor as well as the publisher. The reader whose paper has an ombudsman enjoys an 85 percent chance of having that paper edited by someone who gets an "A" rating from the publisher for ethics. For the reader of a paper without an ombudsman, the probability drops to 60 percent.

What, finally, do these data tell us beyond the obvious fact that the variety of editors, publishers, their operating arrangements, and their ethical outcomes is great? How can we evaluate these results? How can editors and publishers use them to improve their own ethical efficiency? It is almost time to attempt to answer those questions. But first we must decide what we mean by "ethical efficiency."

PART SIX

Toward Ethical Efficiency

We start with several assumptions. The first is that news people are men and women of good will who want to do the right thing. They do not need to be preached to, and exhortation to behave more ethically would be neither needed nor very much heeded. What people in the news business can use, however, is some help in implementing and articulating their own already high standards. The formal study of ethics has, since the days of Socrates, Plato, and Aristotle, aimed not at turning bad people into good but in helping good people to understand and realize their goodness. We are all victims of our own haste. We make evaluations too quickly, often thoughtlessly, and without the critical self-examination that would tell us if the path we are on really takes us where we want to go. The ethically efficient person is persistent enough to carry his evaluations beyond snap judgments and easy conventions.

Chicago Tribune columnist Bob Greene agonized in public after he decided to cooperate with the FBI and write a column designed to trap the Tylenol killer ("Trying to Trap the Tylenol Killer: A Columnist's Conscience," ASNE Bulletin, March, 1983). The conventional rule in recent times has been that a reporter should not cooperate with law enforcement officials. The conventional rule was not a good fit in this case. Such rules are generally formed as means to certain ends, and this one grew out of the need to report objectively on oppressive law enforcement tactics during the civil rights and anti-war movements of the 1960s. One of the problems with such rules is that they can become so ingrained that they become ends in themselves, persisting long after the original reason for making them is forgotten. Their blind, reflexive application is not ethically efficient.

Greene was not sure that he behaved ethically. A philosopher who wrote about ethics in the modern world nearly a generation ago would say that he did. "Any attempt to straighten out the relationship between what is valued for its own sake and what is not," said Wayne A. R. Leys, "may be called ethics." (*Ethics and Social Policy*, 1941) At considerable cost in mental and emotional effort, Greene looked behind the conventional rule to discover what he really valued.

Not all news people do that. A few editors in this survey, a very few, asserted that they had no ethical dilemmas because they always knew what to do, always had a policy for everything. That may be efficient in terms of saving time and getting the day's work done, but it is not ethically efficient.

And that brings us to a definition. An ethically efficient news operation will provide an environment where decision makers have the time, the support, and the emotional capital to discover what they really value, to "straighten out the relationship between what is valued for its own sake and what is not."

Can it be measured? Not directly and not easily. So much is hidden from view. But this survey reveals some outcroppings that are subject to measurement. Considering only those things which were measured in this project, the ethically efficient newspaper might show the following:

1. Some degree of freedom from knee-jerk responses. People who always follow the conventional rule may think they are being ethical when in fact they are being thoughtless.

2. Mutual respect between editor and publisher. If the newspaper is ethically efficient, the editor and publisher will know it, and they will like each other for it.

3. High staff morale. News people are in this business for psychic income as much as any other kind. Nothing can destroy morale as much as a perception that the place is being run without regard for moral values.

On each of these counts, as the previous chapter has shown, the newspaper whose publisher takes an active (and non-malign) role on the news side comes out measurably ahead. This does not mean that such a publisher has a monopoly on ethical efficiency, only that it happens more often when he or she is in charge.

Such a finding runs clearly counter to the traditional belief that business and news operations ought to be kept widely separated. But this separation may be another example of a means to a good end which has outlived its usefulness. In its extreme form, journalistic ethics are the sole responsibility of what Norman Isaacs has called the "tribal-craft culture" of the newsroom while outsiders—and the publisher is considered an outsider—are excluded from the process of setting values ("It's Up to Editors to Close the Credibility Gap," *presstime*, February, 1983).

To those of us who inhabited newsrooms where the doctrine of separation prevailed, we were in charge of ethics, and the business side was in charge of just about everything else. We were the good and altruistic guys; they were greedy and wore black hats. They had the grubby job of pursuing the company's economic self-interest. Ours was the nobler task of looking out for the community's welfare. The adversarial model, by which so many activities in American life have been defined, fit even the activities within a single economic unit, the daily newspaper.

One activity seemed to justify the other. The editorial side was free and unfettered in its pursuit of truth and justice because it didn't have to dirty its hands with economic matters. Conversely, the business side could be uninhibited in its quest for profit because the public interest was somebody else's department. The adversarial model has an appealing symmetry to it, and it may have made life easier for both sides, but some newspaper people eventually began to notice that the news side wasn't winning too many close decisions. In the crunch, power rested with the side that controlled the purse strings. And the editors who did the most for their papers were persons who learned the business side of newspapering well enough to get some control of that purse.

In recent years, economic pressures on newspapers have forced many of them to begin to reject internal adversarial activity for a more efficient cooperative mode. In this mode, the business side recognizes that it cannot sell advertising without readers, and that it cannot get and keep readers without a quality editorial product. Some newspaper people still snort at the notion of calling a newspaper a product—despite the fact that it requires capital investment, a manufacturing process, a sales and delivery system, and willing customers in order to exist. But the most effective editors have always known that readers are customers who vote with their quarters and provide a healthy check on the power center that has fewer checks than most. Some editors still fear that participating in business decisions will make them so profit-conscious that they will cease to be advocates for the public good. (For an eloquent expression of that view, see Charles W. Bailey's "Exit Lines from a Minnesota Editor" in *Washington Journalism Review*, January/February, 1983.) Others believe that participation will enable them to play a more effective role in directing the newspaper's resources toward public benefit. Our survey indicates that the latter is becoming the prevailing view. Its logic says that editing a newspaper is an economic activity, and editors who ignore the economic aspect risk sacrificing their ability to harness the full power of the organization on behalf of their readers and their community.

If the adversarial model is inefficient for newspaper economics, can it work efficiently for newspaper ethics? Should ethical outputs be a resultant force created by the clash of opposing interests? The concept is more traditional than it is logical. If there is one ethical code for the business side and a conflicting code for the news side, the net ethical output is likely to be unpredictable at best, and a system without consistency and predictability can hardly be called a system at all. We should consider the possibility that a newspaper's ethical responsibility ought to apply to the organization as a whole and is not something to be subdivided among competing elements. As newspaper managers come to understand the need for economic integrity, the time may be ripe for an appreciation of the need for ethical wholeness.

The model for such an organization is the newspaper whose publisher fits the category we have labeled "Statesman." This is the publisher who is an active participant on the news side for the sole purpose of making it better. His ethical standards are respected by his editor, his news staff is happy, and his responses to specific situations are just difficult enough to pigeonhole to convince us that he approaches ethical problems with thought and logic rather than reflex.

Some editors will cringe at this suggestion, and rightly so, for it can be taken as an invitation for publishers who do not meddle in the news side now to get directly involved. The outcome of such a change would depend very much on the kind of people they are. Perhaps Statesmen are born and not made, and perhaps the publisher who tries to change his behavior to become one will only make matters worse. Perhaps the kind of luck a newspaper has when its publisher is selected is the only important variable. Perhaps.

It is worth remembering, however, that the Statesman, like the other three over-simplified publisher types, is a construct invented for the convenience of the analyst. Real-life publishers fall not into discrete categories so much as they reside on a series of continuous scales. Even the lowliest Partisan has some qualities of the Statesman, and the line between the two can be thin and arbitrary. Any publisher can move in any direction on any scale, and every one has the potential to become more statesmanlike than he or she already is.

The key goal is to put the entire weight and majesty of the newspaper behind its ethical decisions and not to dilute those decisions by partitioning them off to different segments. A newspaper can never be the centrally directed monolith which the public often perceives, but the public is right in holding the newspaper as a whole responsible for what appears or fails to appear on the printed page. "That's not my department," is not an ethical response.

How can a newspaper consolidate its ethical responsibilities?

One way would be to appoint an outside committee, a board of advisors, composed of local citizens representing a broad array of interest groups to sit down with the managers on both news and business sides to evaluate their work from an ethical standpoint. Such a committee might fulfill the same sort of function that an outside director does on the board of a corporation, offering a concerned but detached view which insiders cannot provide. By looking at the newspaper's performance as a whole, this committee might encourage all departments of the paper to work together toward common goals.

Another possibility, not inconsistent with the idea of a board of advisors, would be to work toward internal consolidation of ethical evaluations. This thought is more radical, but it could be quite effective in cracking the insularity of the newsroom, and there is some precedent for it. At many newspapers, integration of economic activity came through the formation of readership committees which brought all of the departments together to focus on the common aim of building and retaining readership. Perhaps the same pattern could be followed to create ethics committees. If business and news sides were to meet to talk about the things they do in terms of ethical standards, each would bring something useful to the table and each might stand to benefit.

For the business side, the benefit could be an increased appreciation for the need for the historic newsroom codes which have stressed accuracy, fairness, and independence. The specific function of many of these codes has been to counter business office pressure in behalf of what Ben Bagdikian has described as "built-in sacred cows, a news bias in favor of the overwhelming conservatism of the country's editorial pages and a chamber-of-commerce set of mind that kept them silent on serious community problems and on consumer maltreatment" (ASNE Bulletin, Jan., 1971). Bagdikian was talking mainly about standards of the 1940's and 1950's, and standards have improved since then, but problems still persist. And concern for ethics belongs on the business side as much as it does in the news-editorial departments. Sensitizing the business side to newsroom ethical concerns could be an important objective for newspaper ethics committees.

One news-side benefit from such committee activity might be an overcoming of the business-aversion reflex which can cloud ethical judgment. Another might be an increased sensitivity to community needs. This lack of sensitivity can be manifested in something as simple as bad manners (Charles Stafford in *presstime*, February, 1983) or as complicated as a set of world views based on near-total cynicism. Admittedly, news people encounter a lot to be cynical about, but if the adversary model is over-generalized to the point where a newspaper staff measures its success in terms of the number of evildoers jailed or public officials discredited, the newspaper risks damaging both itself and the system within which it operates. In the extreme case, a newspaper may abandon standards of fairness and balance—which are basically procedural standards—in favor of a performance standard, with performance measured in terms of damage inflicted upon the intended target. The goal then becomes to effect that damage at all costs. The abandonment of fairness is one of the potential costs. The need for editorial-side people to discuss and even defend their actions in a company-wide committee might promote more introspection and reflection. The object would not be to reverse the standards of skeptical inquiry but to remain true to them, knowing, as Michael J. O'Neill told ASNE in May, 1982, that "in its more extreme forms, the adversarial attitude creates barriers to the clear observation and analysis necessary for objectivity."

And this could be the point of an all-newspaper ethics committee: not to challenge basic values so much as to bring clarity of observation and analysis to bear on problems that might otherwise be treated in some less considered fashion. While a committee clearly should not attempt to keep up with day-to-day decision making, it could discuss specific cases from the recent past and compare what was done with the options that were rejected. Authority cannot be effectively delegated to an intradepartmental committee, but such a body could serve as a useful device for surfacing and examining questions that might otherwise go unexamined.

Some editors might reasonably object to such a plan on the grounds that a newspaper-wide ethics committee would give the controllers of the purse strings undesirable access to newsroom decision-making. They might be right. However, the power of money tends to assert itself in one way or another in spite of institutional barriers, and the committee might serve to ventilate power relationships that had been covert. A strong editor could use the committee to promote his or her own ideals and muster support that was not available before.

Another trade-off for the editor would be the opportunity to approach as ethical issues questions not previously on his or her agenda. For example, how much of the wealth which a newspaper takes out of a community is it morally obligated to give back in services? What non-journalistic activities are appropriate for a newspaper company? What limits should a publisher put on his involvement in civic activity? What kinds of advertising are inappropriate? When a committee looks at the organization's total ethical outputs, editors could help guide it to a moral consistency not attainable when the questions are fragmented and attacked in isolation.

Publishers might reasonably object to putting such questions to an ethical test when they are already quite complicated as business questions. In the long run, however, business issues and ethical issues may not be separable. A newspaper, as most publishers well know, exists at the sufferance of the community it serves. The customers who buy the newspaper and support its advertisers do so by choice, and that choice must be renewed every day. As national readership figures show, many people are not making that renewal. The proportion of people who say they read a newspaper every day took another drop in 1982, reaching a record low of 54 percent, according to the National Opinion Research Center of the University of Chicago which has been making periodic measurements since 1967. That first measurement showed the proportion of daily readers in the adult population to be 73 percent, and it has been lower with each succeeding measurement. The same survey shows confidence in people running the press to be at an all-time low. The confidence question has been asked eight times since 1973, and last year, for the first time, the people who said they have "hardly any" confidence in the press's leadership outnumbered those who had "a great deal" of confidence. (The confidence question has also been asked by the Harris Survey with somewhat different results. For a summary of the Harris numbers from 1966 to 1982, see the article by Maxwell E. McCombs and Laura Washington in the February, 1983, *presstime*.) Here is that trend as measured by NORC:

I am going to name some institutions in this country. As far as the people running these institutions are concerned, would you say you have a great deal of confidence, only some confidence, or hardly any confidence at all in them?

Confidence in the Press

	1973	1974	1975	1976	1977	1978	1980	1982
A great deal	23%	26%	24%	28%	25%	20%	22%	18%
Some	61	55	55	52	57	58	58	59
Hardly any	15	17	18	18	15	20	17	21
Don't know	2	1	3	2	2	2	3	2

As a very minimum, the industry has a public relations problem which no prudent business person can ignore. The advantage of treating the newspaper's impact on its community in an ethical framework instead of from a public relations perspective is that the ethical approach requires action at a more basic level and earlier in time, before problems ever reach a PR level. The PR approach explains and justifies what we do. The ethical approach helps us decide what to do. And it might even make us feel better.

If there were a committee formed to try to integrate a newspaper's ethical approach, what should be on its agenda? Despite the obvious difficulties with ethical codes for journalists, writing, or attempting to write, a code might be a useful activity for such a committee. The variety of problems that newspapers face is so great that journalists may always have to be situation ethicists. James C. Thomson Jr., who earns his living by associating with off-duty journalists as curator of the Nieman Foundation, has expressed the problem well. "The ambiguities of journalism are too endemic and ineradicable, its domain too wide and infinitely varied," he says (*Nieman Reports*, Winter/Spring, 1978). But even situation ethics requires some structure within which alternatives are evaluated. Moreover, most of the journalists in this survey claim to be code ethicists. The question was put to them directly, as described in Part Five of this report, and 59 percent of the nation's newspaper readers have publishers and 63 percent have editors and staff members who believe in working by a written code. Even when the question was put more generally, there was about the same level of agreement that ethical questions should be decided according "to certain universal truths about right and wrong which never change."

About half the reading population is served by papers that have written codes of ethics already—with editors and publishers more likely to be aware of these codes than staff members. And these codes are referred to, or at least kept in a convenient place, because, among readers whose papers have codes, 91 percent have editors who say they could put their hands on them without having to look around to find them.

Given that codes cannot be written to cover all situations, they can surely at least be used to denote a sensitivity to certain values and desires. Every decision involves a trade-off, and sometimes the trade is between one ethical value and another. News people make trade-offs more often than many outsiders may suspect. The recurring issue of preserving confidentiality of sources is an example. Most of us believe that a person accused of crime has a right to compel testimony on his or her behalf. We also believe that a reporter has a duty to keep a promise to conceal a source. When the reporter's promise stands between the defendant and testimony that would help him, one precept or the other has to yield. It will come as a surprise to many people that sometimes it is the reporter's code that yields—and it would be hard to argue that there are never times when it should. Indeed, the absolutist position on confidentiality pledges is a minority view, held by editors and publishers representing only about one fifth of the total readership.

Minority hiring is another everyday example. Although the subject was not covered in the survey, there is ample anecdotal evidence that newspaper managers believe in hiring without regard to race and that they often suspend that belief in order to increase minority representation on the staff. A procedural code clashes with a performance standard, and something has to yield.

The fact that codes are bent does not mean that they are useless. Even the act of bending can serve as a reminder that they exist and that an ethical judgment is rooted in a fixed value system from which all departures are measured.

For newspaper people, the process of code creation can itself heighten awareness of ethical issues, and its existence can clarify thinking about the trade-offs. Even an enigmatic code might be of some use in that sense. And it would be an excellent agenda-setting device for an ethics committee, especially as existing codes of other organizations are examined and compared to the newspaper's own experiences, and as discussion is generated. Getting ethical issues to the level of consciousness where they are discussed may be the most difficult task of all. It may also be the most important task.

Frequencies

The tables on the following pages show the frequencies for each of the questions asked in the survey. Percentages are based on circulation as explained in the introduction to this report. Numbers in parentheses show how many newspaper responses contributed to the percentages in the column headed "total." These numbers are not completely weighted for circulation and will therefore vary somewhat from the percentage figures. Because information was sought from a publisher, an editor, and a staff member, there is a potential for three responses from each paper.

ASNE Survey on Newspaper Ethics

Part One: Editors Only

V005. Does this market have just one daily newspaper or is there more than one?

Only one	27%	(113)
More than one	73%	(211)

V006. (If more than one) Does your company own more than one paper in this market?

Yes	43%	(97)
No	57%	(112)

V007. (If company owns more than one) Are you the editor for just one paper, or more than one?

One	64%	(53)
More	36%	(46)

V008. Does the publisher live in your circulation area or does he/she live somewhere else?

In area	94%	(303)
Somewhere else	6%	(19)

V009. Does the company which owns your newspaper(s) also own news-papers in other markets, or is this the only one?

Owns others	78%	(242)
Only one	22%	(82)

V010. Is the company privately owned, or is its stock traded publicly?

Privately owned	68%	(232)
Stock traded	32%	(92)

V011. Does your paper have a regular ombudsman column?

Yes	15%	(36)
No	85%	(288)

V012. (If regular column) Is the ombudsman chosen by you or by someone independent of you?

By editor	58%	(23)
By someone else	36%	(8)
Written by editor	7%	(3)

V013. (If regular column) Do you read the ombudsman's copy before it is published?

Yes	37%	(15)
No	63%	(16)

V014. (If regular column) Do you read it for information or to approve it?

Information	89%	(10)
Approve	11%	(2)

V015. I am going to read a list of different ways that newspapers handle corrections and amplifications. Please tell me which one comes closest to your paper's policy.

   1. Corrections appear under a standing head, anchored to a specific place in the paper.

2. Corrections appear under a standing head which floats as needed.

3. Corrections are run as needed, without a standing head or a particular location in the paper.

4. Corrections are normally not made. The most we'll do is run another version of the story to get a correct version in the paper, but without acknowledging that it is a correction.

5. No correction of any kind is made.

Statement 1	55%	(171)
Statement 2	21%	(67)
Statement 3	24%	(82)
Statement 4	0%	(1)
Statement 5	0%	(1)

I am going to read a list of ethical questions that newspapers sometimes face. For each one, I would like you to estimate how often cases of that type are discussed at your paper. The first type of ethical question involves . . .

V016. News gathering methods—using false identity; stolen documents; concealed recording; eavesdropping.

Never	28%	(106)
Less than once a year	19%	(59)
About once or twice a year	28%	(76)
Several times a year	18%	(52)
About once a month	4%	(10)
2-3 times a month	2%	(5)
Nearly every week	2%	(4)
Several times a week	0%	(1)

V017. Protection of sources granting and preserving confidentiality; disguising the nature of a source with a vested interest or otherwise withholding relevant information from the reader.

Never	6%	(23)
Less than once a year	8%	(28)
About once or twice a year	16%	(61)
Several times a year	35%	(111)
About once a month	16%	(39)
2-3 times a month	9%	(24)
Nearly every week	7%	(20)
Several times a week	4%	(9)

V018. Invasion of privacy: causing injury to feelings; disclosing embarrassing private facts.

Never	5%	(14)
Less than once a year	8%	(25)
About once or twice a year	16%	(53)
Several times a year	33%	(106)
About once a month	18%	(44)
2-3 times a month	12%	(34)
Nearly every week	6%	(21)
Several times a week	3%	(7)

V019. Economic temptations: accepting trips, meals, favors, loans, gifts, from sources or suppliers, or heavy socializing with sources.

Never	28%	(91)
Less than once a year	10%	(27)
About once or twice a year	31%	(95)
Several times a year	18%	(58)
About once a month	12%	(29)
2-3 times a month	1%	(4)
Nearly every week	1%	(2)
Several times a week	1%	(2)

V020. Government secrecy: grand jury leaks; national security problems, including military secrets and diplomatic leaks.

Never	15%	(61)
Less than once a year	14%	(50)
About once or twice a year	32%	(99)
Several times a year	21%	(66)
About once a month	12%	(21)
2-3 times a month	2%	(8)
Nearly every week	2%	(4)
Several times a week	2%	(4)

V021. Civil disorder: publicizing rioters, terrorists, bomb threats, at the risk of encouraging imitators.

Never	13%	(47)
Less than once a year	26%	(66)
About once or twice a year	32%	(102)
Several times a year	24%	(73)
About once a month	3%	(8)
2-3 times a month	3%	(6)
Nearly every week	1%	(2)
Several times a week	0%	(0)

V022. Photos: violence, obscenity, hurt feelings.

Never	9%	(20)
Less than once a year	4%	(15)
About once or twice a year	19%	(65)
Several times a year	39%	(113)
About once a month	14%	(49)
2-3 times a month	5%	(15)
Nearly every week	6%	(21)
Several times a week	4%	(7)

V023. Pressure from advertisers: blurbs, business office musts, keeping things out of the paper or getting them in.

Never	21%	(59)
Less than once a year	6%	(18)
About once or twice a year	26%	(73)
Several times a year	20%	(68)
About once a month	11%	(38)
2-3 times a month	6%	(18)
Nearly every week	6%	(24)
Several times a week	3%	(12)

V024. Fairness, balance and objectivity: allocating space to opposing interest groups or political candidates. Providing right of reply to criticism.

Never	2%	(9)
Less than once a year	2%	(9)
About once or twice a year	6%	(20)
Several times a year	25%	(82)
About once a month	15%	(52)
2-3 times a month	13%	(35)
Nearly every week	14%	(53)
Several times a week	22%	(51)

V025. Conflict of interests: interest group activity by editors and publishers; service on boards and committees; campaign donations; stories involving financial interests of newspaper staff or management; spouse involvement.

Never	17%	(49)
Less than once a year	16%	(44)
About once or twice a year	38%	(116)
Several times a year	22%	(71)
About once a month	4%	(17)
2-3 times a month	2%	(6)
Nearly every week	1%	(2)
Several times a week	1%	(2)

V026. Use of reporters for non-news tasks: writing advertising supplements, gathering data for the company's financial decisions or labor relations objectives.

Never	62%	(192)
Less than once a year	15%	(40)
About once or twice a year	15%	(50)
Several times a year	7%	(23)
About once a month	1%	(5)
2-3 times a month	0%	(0)
Nearly every week	1%	(5)
Several times a week	0%	(0)

V027. Suppression of news to protect the community, factory relocations, school closings, highway expansion, etc.

Never	55%	(159)
Less than once a year	12%	(39)
About once or twice a year	18%	(56)
Several times a year	5%	(19)
About once a month	8%	(28)
2-3 times a month	1%	(5)
Nearly every week	2%	(5)
Several times a week	0%	(0)

Part Two: Publishers, Editors and Staff Members

V029. Have you seen the movie, "Absence of Malice"?

	Publishers	Editors	Staff Members	Total	
Yes	54%	54%	50%	53%	(357)
No	46	46	50	47	(373)

V030. (IF YES TO V029) Which of the following four statements about "Absence of Malice" comes closest to the way you, yourself, feel about the movie?

a. The movie gives an accurate portrayal of problems that sometimes occur in the newspaper business.

b. The movie made some valid points about problems in the newspaper business, but it does so with situations that were exaggerated and not true to life.

c. The situations and people in the movie bore hardly any resemblance to the newspaper business as I know it, and its moral points have little value.

d. The movie was an unfair and inaccurate attack on the newspaper profession.

	Publishers	Editors	Staff Members	Total
Statement a	25%	21%	18%	22% (72)
Statement b	63	70	76	70 (254)
Statement c	9	9	4	8 (27)
Statement d	3	0	1	1 (3)

V031. Was any formal action taken in response to "Absence of Malice" at your newspaper in the way of discussion groups, committees, or actions to put ethics on your policy agenda?

	Publishers	Editors	Staff Members	Total
Yes	8%	9%	4%	7% (50)
No	92	91	96	93 (662)

V032. (IF YES TO V031) Was that action based more on the publisher's initiative or more on the editor's initiative?

	Publishers	Editors	Staff Members	Total
Publisher's	62%	7%	10%	26% (15)
Editor's	38	93	90	74 (34)

V033. Newspapers vary greatly in the amount of involvement that publishers have in the news operations. Here are four statements describing different levels of publisher involvement. Regardless of how things work at your paper, which of the following statements comes closest to describing the way you think *publishers* ought to operate:

   a. The publisher should always be involved in deciding what appears in his or her newspaper on a day-to-day basis.

   b. The publisher should generally be involved in deciding what appears in his or her newspaper over the long run, but not on a daily basis.

   c. The publisher should be involved in hiring good people to run the news operation, but not in deciding what appears in the paper; his only intervention in the news operation should be to hire or fire the editor. ·

   d. The publisher should have nothing whatever to do with the news operation.

	Publishers	Editors	Staff Members	Total
Statement a	4%	2%	1%	2% (18)
Statement b	79	58	54	63 (465)
Statement c	18	36	43	32 (229)
Statement d	0	5	2	3 (16)

V034. Now that you have told us how publishers *should* operate, please indicate which of the four comes closest to the way things actually work at your paper.

a. The publisher is always involved in deciding what appears in his or her newspaper on a day-to-day basis.

b. The publisher is generally involved in deciding what appears in the newspaper over the long run, but not on a daily basis.

c. The publisher is involved in hiring good people to run the news operation, but not in deciding what appears in the paper; his only intervention in the news operation is to hire or fire the editor.

d. The publisher has nothing whatever to do with the news operation.

	Publishers	Editors	Staff Members	Total
Statement a	5%	3%	9%	5% (42)
Statement b	74	61	53	63 (465)
Statement c	21	32	29	27 (181)
Statement d	0	4	9	5 (33)

V035. One issue in some companies is how much editors should be involved in the company's marketing and financial plans. Which of the following statements best describes the role you think the *editor* should have at your company?

a. The editor should participate fully in financial planning and marketing decisions.

b. The editor should be kept fully informed in financial planning and marketing decisions, but should participate only when questions related to his specific expertise are involved.

c. The editor should be kept informed of financial planning and marketing decisions on a "need-to-know" basis, i.e. whenever his help is needed in carrying out the decisions.

d. The editor should be insulated from all financial planning and marketing decisions so that he can concentrate on putting out the paper.

	Publishers	Editors	Staff Members	Total
Statement a	42%	45%	20%	36% (239)
Statement b	34	39	54	43 (340)
Statement c	23	14	21	19 (132)
Statement d	1	2	6	3 (19)

V036. Which comes closest to describing the actual situation at your company?

a. The editor participates fully in financial planning and marketing decisions.

b. The editor is kept fully informed in financial planning and marketing decisions.

c. The editor is kept informed of financial planning and marketing decisions on a "need-to-know" basis, i.e. whenever his help is needed in carrying out the decisions.

    d. The editor is insulated from all financial planning and marketing decisions so that he can concentrate on putting out the paper.

	Publishers	Editors	Staff Members	Total	
Statement a	27%	28%	11%	22%	(162)
Statement b	38	33	38	36	(259)
Statement c	34	35	45	38	(270)
Statement d	1	4	6	4	(29)

V037. Newspaper people have different ideas about respecting pledges of confidentiality. Which of the following statements comes closest to your view:

    a. A pledge of confidentiality to a source should always be kept no matter what the circumstances, even if it means a long jail term for the reporter and heavy financial cost to the newspaper.

    b. A pledge of confidentiality should always be taken seriously, but it can be violated in unusual circumstances, as when it is learned the source lied to the reporter.

    c. A pledge of confidentiality can be broken if the editor and the reporter agree that the harm done by keeping it is greater than the damage caused by breaking it.

    d. Pledges of confidentiality are largely rhetorical devices and not intended to be taken seriously.

	Publishers	Editors	Staff Members	Total	
Statement a	18%	20%	40%	25%	(179)
Statement b	65	71	51	62	(447)
Statement c	18	9	9	12	(99)
Statement d	0	0	0	0	(2)

V038. Under which of the following circumstances should a newspaper publish material from leaked grand jury transcripts:

    a. Whenever the material is newsworthy.

    b. Whenever the importance of the material revealed outweighs the damage to the system from breaching of its security.

    c. Only if the material exposes flaws in the workings of the grand jury system itself, e.g., it shows the prosecutor to be acting improperly.

    d. Never.

	Publishers	Editors	Staff Members	Total	
Statement a	11%	19%	32%	20%	(145)
Statement b	62	60	49	57	(396)
Statement c	23	15	13	17	(140)
Statement d	3	7	7	6	(42)

V039. A reporter is assigned to find out about the activities of a political action group whose objectives are in sharp contrast to his own strongly held views. To get the story he needs the cooperation of group members. Should the reporter:

a. Ask the editor to assign someone else to the story.

b. Take care to explain his own views to the sources so that they can take them into account in deciding how to deal with him.

c. Keep quiet about his own views, but be frank and forthcoming if asked.

d. Adopt the stance of a sympathetic neutral.

e. Pose as an advocate of the action group's objectives.

	Publishers	Editors	Staff Members	Total	
Statement a	28%	35%	16%	26%	(200)
Statement b	5	1	1	2	(20)
Statement c	53	45	53	50	(360)
Statement d	15	20	29	21	(145)
Statement e	0	0	0	0	(0)

V040. The first refugees from the Falkland Islands come to stay with relatives in your town. You know from the Iranian hostage experience that they are likely to be harrassed and intimidated by competing news persons striving for the last detail. Already, reporters and camera persons are setting up camp in their front yard. Should the editor:

a. Organize pool coverage to reduce the burden on the family.

b. Make a public plea for all media to use restraint.

c. Avoid public pronouncements, but order his own staff to use restraint.

d. Do nothing, on the theory that competitive news coverage is best for society in the long run.

	Publishers	Editors	Staff Members	Total	
Statement a	8%	7%	16%	10%	(86)
Statement b	4	4	2	3	(31)
Statement c	65	70	51	62	(447)
Statement d	23	20	31	24	(164)

V041. A prominent citizen is vacationing alone in Key West, and his hotel burns down. The wire service story lists him among those who escaped uninjured and identifies the hotel as a popular gathering place for affluent gays. The citizen says he'll commit suicide if you publish his name in the story. Should the editor:

a. Publish the story in full.

b. Publish the story, but without mentioning the gay angle.

c. Publish the story, but without mentioning the local citizen.
d. Kill the story.

	Publishers	Editors	Staff Members	Total
Statement a	39%	41%	46%	42% (286)
Statement b	50	52	43	49 (370)
Statement c	10	7	10	9 (65)
Statement d	1	0	0	0 (4)

V042. In making the decision indicated above, who should be involved?
a. The editor only.
b. The editor, in consultation with the publisher.
c. The publisher, in consultation with the editor.
d. The publisher only.

	Publishers	Editors	Staff Members	Total
Statement a	39%	60%	57%	52% (339)
Statement b	50	38	39	42 (344)
Statement c	11	2	4	6 (50)
Statement d	0	0	0	0 (0)

V043. An investigative reporter uses a computer to analyze criminal court records and writes a prize-winning series. A major computer manufacturer then offers to pay him $500 to speak at a seminar for reporters which it is sponsoring at a university. Which of the following best describes your view?
a. The reporter should be allowed to make the speech and accept the $500 from the computer manufacturer.
b. The reporter should be allowed to make the speech, but accept the $500 only if the honorarium is paid through the university.
c. The reporter should be allowed to make the speech but not to accept the honorarium.
d. The reporter should not be allowed to make the speech.

	Publishers	Editors	Staff Members	Total
Statement a	28%	24%	38%	30% (232)
Statement b	19	18	16	17 (147)
Statement c	48	51	41	47 (310)
Statement d	5	8	5	6 (43)

V044. In making the decision indicated above, who should be involved?
a. The editor only.
b. The editor, in consultation with the publisher.
c. The publisher, in consultation with the editor.
d. The publisher only.

	Publishers	Editors	Staff Members	Total	
Statement a	37%	72%	76%	62%	(422)
Statement b	50	27	20	32	(258)
Statement c	12	2	4	6	(49)
Statement d	1	0	1	1	(5)

V045. An investigative reporter discovers a former city employee now living in another state who has evidence of a kickback scheme involving the mayor and half the city council. He appears interested in cooperating with your investigation, but indicates that he will want money. Should your paper:

a. Pay an honorarium based on the news value of the story.

b. Put him on the payroll for the time that he spends working with your staff in gathering and documenting the facts, plus expenses.

c. Pay his out-of-pocket expenses only.

d. Pay nothing.

	Publishers	Editors	Staff Members	Total	
Statement a	8%	7%	4%	6%	(49)
Statement b	14	5	7	8	(65)
Statement c	33	32	33	33	(226)
Statement d	46	56	56	53	(392)

V046. An investigative reporter does a thorough and praiseworthy expose of inequalities in tax assessment practices. In the course of investigating for the story, he looks at his own assessment records and finds that a value-enhancing addition to his property was never recorded, and as a result, his taxes are $300 less than they should be. He reports this fact in the first draft of his story, but, later, at the urging of his wife, takes it out. Should the editor:

a. Insist that he leave the information in, even though it will raise the reporter's taxes.

b. Talk to the wife and try to persuade her that the reporter's honesty at leaving it in will be rewarded, someday.

c. Leave it to the reporter to decide, but appeal to his conscience.

d. Don't interfere.

	Publishers	Editors	Staff Members	Total	
Statement a	63%	74%	58%	65%	(456)
Statement b	2	4	2	3	(23)
Statement c	29	17	29	25	(184)
Statement d	6	5	11	7	(58)

V047. A just-nominated presidential candidate is meeting with state party chairpersons to discuss his choice for vice presidential candidate. The meeting is closed to the press. A reporter, pretending to be a party staff person, hands a briefcase to one of the people going into the meeting and asks him to leave it on the table for his boss. The briefcase contains a tape recorder, and the reporter retrieves it after the meeting. Should the editor:

    a. Admonish the reporter and kill the story.

    b. Admonish the reporter, but use the information as background for conventional reporting.

    c. Admonish the reporter, but use the story.

    d. Reward the reporter and use the story.

	Publishers	Editors	Staff Members	Total	
Statement a	40%	45%	43%	43%	(332)
Statement b	45	29	32	35	(255)
Statement c	3	7	5	5	(32)
Statement d	12	20	20	17	(103)

V048. Suppose the meeting was of the local party central committee. Which action should the editor take?

    a. Admonish the reporter and kill the story.

    b. Admonish the reporter, but use the information as background for conventional reporting.

    c. Admonish the reporter, but use the story.

    d. Reward the reporter and use the story.

	Publishers	Editors	Staff Members	Total	
Statement a	41%	45%	43%	43%	(340)
Statement b	43	28	32	34	(248)
Statement c	4	7	6	6	(37)
Statement d	12	20	19	17	(101)

V049. The city manager has proposed a one-way street plan which adds a mile and a half to the route your newspaper's circulation trucks must take to reach the major freeways. The circulation manager proposes an alternate plan, and top management agrees to have the company's lawyer present it to city council. In covering the story, should the editor:

    a. Give no special instructions to the city desk.

    b. Tell the desk to cover the story fully, and take special precautions to get the facts straight.

    c. Have a free-lance writer, whose livelihood does not depend on the paper, cover the story.

d. Use the wire story.

	Publishers	Editors	Staff Members	Total	
Statement a	27%	32%	41%	33%	(258)
Statement b	72	66	57	65	(458)
Statement c	1	1	1	1	(9)
Statement d	1	1	1	1	(8)

V050. In making the decision indicated above, who should be involved?
   a. The editor only.
   b. The editor, in consultation with the publisher.
   c. The publisher, in consultation with the editor.
   d. The publisher only.

	Publishers	Editors	Staff Members	Total	
Statement a	50%	71%	73%	65%	(459)
Statement b	40	27	25	31	(236)
Statement c	10	2	2	4	(37)
Statement d	0	0	0	0	(2)

V051. The company that owns a major metropolitan newspaper also owns a major sports franchise in that town. Should the paper:
   a. Try to build up local interest in the team it owns, because it is good for community spirit as well as profitable to the company.
   b. Treat the team exactly as it treats any other team.
   c. Bend over backwards to be fair and treat the company-owned team with more skepticism and outright criticism than are accorded other teams.
   d. Sell the franchise.

	Publishers	Editors	Staff Members	Total	
Statement a	2%	3%	3%	3%	(20)
Statement b	80	79	70	77	(560)
Statement c	3	0	1	1	(7)
Statement d	15	18	26	20	(141)

V052. The business manager of the company has developed close friendships with Canadian newsprint suppliers, reinforced by regular hunting trips in the north woods as their guest. The company decides to prohibit managers from accepting favors from suppliers. The business manager continues to take the trips. Should the publisher:
   a. Fire the business manager.
   b. Impose discipline short of firing and extract a promise that it will not happen again.

c. Advise the business manager to pay his own way on these trips or reciprocate by hosting the suppliers on equivalent outings.

d. Decide that the no-favor rule should not apply to such longstanding and clearly benign activities.

	Publishers	Editors	Staff Members	Total
Statement a	20%	28%	18%	22% (145)
Statement b	58	51	48	52 (391)
Statement c	17	18	32	22 (169)
Statement d	5	3	2	3 (23)

V053. Your company receives a special rate from a major hotel chain for your traveling employees. A staff member goes out of town for a three-day business meeting and, because the site of the meeting is a major cultural center, decides to stay through the week at his own expense. He pays his own hotel bill for Friday and Saturday nights, but at the special commercial rate. Your company has a conflict of interest policy against employees accepting any kind of favor or reward from suppliers. Should your company:

a. Fire the traveling employee.

b. Require him to reimburse the hotel for the difference between the commercial and regular rate and warn him not to repeat the practice.

c. Warn him not to repeat the practice, but not worry about reimbursement because the amount is so small.

d. Make a ruling that such discounts are not considered favors or rewards under the conflict-of-interest policy.

	Publishers	Editors	Staff Members	Total
Statement a	0%	1%	0%	1% (5)
Statement b	24	44	65	44 (347)
Statement c	27	16	14	19 (125)
Statement d	49	40	21	37 (247)

V054. The restaurant reviewer at your paper has become friendly with a local restaurant operator and, working without pay, has helped his friend to design and plan a new restaurant with a continental theme—the exact sort of restaurant whose absence in your town he has decried in his column. Should the editor:

a. Fire the restaurant critic.

b. Admonish the critic not to get so close to sources, and ban any mention of the new restaurant in his column.

c. Advise the critic not to do it again, but take no further action.

d. Do nothing.

	Publishers	Editors	Staff Members	Total	
Statement a	4%	12%	8%	8%	(62)
Statement b	48	58	49	52	(335)
Statement c	32	20	27	26	(204)
Statement d	16	10	16	14	(116)

V055. Easter Sunday is approaching, and the editor plans the traditional page-one recognition of the holiday: A banner, "He Is Risen." Then a new publisher, who happens to be an agnostic, points out that the latest religious census shows the community to be six percent non-Christian. Should the editor:

a. Keep the Easter banner.

b. Reduce the size of the headline in deference to the non-Christians in the community.

c. Limit the paper's coverage to specific religious-oriented events scheduled for that day.

d. Avoid any mention of Easter.

	Publishers	Editors	Staff Members	Total	
Statement a	62%	50%	42%	51%	(398)
Statement b	5	4	4	4	(30)
Statement c	30	46	53	43	(286)
Statement d	3	1	1	2	(9)

V056. What percent non-Christian should the community reach before you would choose a different response?

	Publishers	Editors	Staff Members	Total	
Mean Percent	50.4%	44.4%	47.4%	47.3%	(477)

V057. Your Washington correspondent has spent years developing friendships with the key people now in power, and it is paying off. He knows the town well, and they are relative newcomers, so he is frequently consulted by the White House staff and the President's political operatives before key decisions are made. Should the editor:

a. Fire the Washington correspondent.

b. Move the correspondent to another city.

c. Admonish the Washington correspondent to maintain a reasonable distance from his sources.

d. Reward the Washington correspondent for developing such a good knowledge of his subject and such loyal sources.

	Publishers	Editors	Staff Members	Total	
Statement a	1%	1%	1%	1%	(10)
Statement b	10	6	16	10	(78)

Statement c	75	77	71	75 (521)
Statement d	14	16	12	14 (114)

V058. The publisher is convinced that a downtown amusement park is just what the community needs. The editor of the editorial page opposes it. Should the publisher:

a. Order the editor to support the amusement park.
b. Drop some gentle hints to the editor, but avoid a direct order.
c. Avoid discussing the issue with the editor at all.
d. Encourage the editor to call the issue as he sees it.

	Publishers	Editors	Staff Members	Total
Statement a	35%	29%	15%	26% (192)
Statement b	27	19	15	21 (170)
Statement c	2	3	10	5 (39)
Statement d	36	49	58	48 (312)

V059. A scandal is unfolding in city government, and your paper is getting more than its share of the news beats. But, today, your paper is beaten by a competing medium on a key element of the story. Should your paper:

a. Treat the new element just as though the competition had never mentioned it.
b. Acknowledge the competition's beat in print and cover the story according to its intrinsic news value.
c. Downgrade the importance of the new element.
d. Ignore the new element.

	Publishers	Editors	Staff Members	Total
Statement a	44%	39%	41%	41% (324)
Statement b	56	61	59	59 (406)
Statement c	0	1	0	0 (2)
Statement d	0	0	0	0 (0)

V060. The chief photographer moonlights as a wedding photographer. The father of a bride calls the editor and says the photographer has made a sales pitch to his daughter and included a sly hint that if he is hired for the job, her picture has a better chance of making the society page. The editor investigates and confirms that this is the photographer's regular practice. Should the editor:

a. Fire the photographer.
b. Impose lesser discipline and order the photographer to stop moonlighting.
c. Allow the photographer to continue moonlighting but order him

not to use—or pretend to use—his position to gain favored treatment for clients.

    d. Ask the photographer to be more discreet.

	Publishers	Editors	Staff Members	Total
Statement a	44%	47%	49%	47% (327)
Statement b	13	16	15	15 (116)
Statement c	43	36	37	39 (287)
Statement d	0	0	0	0 (1)

V061. A business writer discovers that TV sets with built-in videotex decoders will be on the local market within 60 days, greatly increasing convenience and reducing costs for people who sign up for the local videotex service—which, incidentally, is not owned by your paper. The advertising manager calls the publisher and says local TV dealers are afraid they will be stuck with an oversupply of obsolete TV sets if the word gets out. Should the publisher:

    a. Order the story killed.

    b. Explain the problem to the editor with a recommendation that the story be delayed.

    c. Suggest to the editor that the story be double-checked for accuracy.

    d. Help the ad manager pacify the retailers, but say nothing to the editor.

	Publishers	Editors	Staff Members	Total
Statement a	0%	0%	0%	0% (0)
Statement b	3	2	2	3 (20)
Statement c	47	36	34	39 (297)
Statement d	50	62	64	59 (405)

V062. A local boy who grew up in poverty makes good by educating himself, working hard, and becoming a successful businessman. This effort culminates in the opening of the fanciest restaurant the town has yet seen. His younger brother has also made good, in a way, by becoming an editorial writer, and he salutes his brother's Horatio Alger story in a folksy and appealing signed column. To ward off any charge of conflict of interest, he identifies himself as the brother of the subject of the piece in the opening paragraph. Should the editor:

    a. Kill the column.

    b. Have the column rewritten to eliminate the brother's name and the name of the restaurant.

    c. Move the piece to some less conspicuous part of the paper.

    d. Let it stand.

	Publishers	Editors	Staff Members	Total
Statement a	23%	22%	20%	21% (128)
Statement b	4	0	4	3 (22)
Statement c	5	3	8	5 (42)
Statement d	68	75	69	71 (535)

V063. Your paper's city hall reporter has gotten so close to the mayor and his staff that they frequently consult him before making major decisions. Should the editor:

    a. Fire the reporter.

    b. Move the reporter to a different beat.

    c. Admonish the reporter to maintain a reasonable distance from his sources.

    d. Reward the reporter for developing such a good knowledge of his subject and such loyal sources.

	Publishers	Editors	Staff Members	Total
Statement a	1%	1%	1%	1% (7)
Statement b	30	21	38	30 (219)
Statement c	61	67	55	61 (428)
Statement d	9	11	6	9 (69)

V064. In making the decision indicated above, who should be involved?

    a. The editor only.

    b. The editor, in consultation with the publisher.

    c. The publisher, in consultation with the editor.

    d. The publisher only.

	Publishers	Editors	Staff Members	Total
Statement a	49%	86%	84%	73% (524)
Statement b	46	15	14	25 (187)
Statement c	4	0	1	2 (17)
Statement d	0	0	0	0 (1)

V065. Some newspaper companies in Florida donated money to a campaign to defeat a statewide referendum which, if passed, would have legalized gambling. Which of the following statements comes closest to your view on this action?

    a. A newspaper that takes an editorial stand on an issue has a right, and possibly even a duty, to back up its belief with its money.

    b. The contributions are justified if the referendum would have a detrimental effect on the business climate in which the newspaper operates.

    c. The contributions should not have been made because they might lead readers to question the objectivity of the papers' news coverage.

    d. No political contributions should ever be made by newspapers;

the news and editorial columns make us powerful enough already, and adding money only indicates inappropriate hunger for more power.

	Publishers	Editors	Staff Members	Total	
Statement a	22%	11%	6%	13%	(105)
Statement b	11	2	4	5	(39)
Statement c	23	31	34	30	(224)
Statement d	44	56	57	53	(347)

V066. If an editor could set any rule he or she wanted for defining the relationship with the publisher, which of the following possible rules would result in the best newspaper?

a. Don't ever talk to me about what I put in the paper.

b. Make suggestions about the content if you want, but don't give orders, unless to fire me.

c. Play a major role in the big decisions—creating new sections, targeting new markets, and major design changes, for example—but don't get involved in individual stories.

d. Be the boss, all the way.

	Publishers	Editors	Staff Members	Total	
Statement a	0%	0%	2%	1%	(5)
Statement b	11	26	36	24	(171)
Statement c	82	72	61	72	(520)
Statement d	8	2	1	4	(33)

V067. Which of the above rules comes closest to describing what actually happens at your newspaper?

a. Don't ever talk to me about what I put in the paper.

b. Make suggestions about the content if you want, but don't give orders, unless to fire me.

c. Play a major role in the big decisions—creating new sections, targeting new markets, and major design changes, for example—but don't get involved in individual stories.

d. Be the boss, all the way.

	Publishers	Editors	Staff Members	Total	
Statement a	0%	2%	2%	1%	(11)
Statement b	13	25	29	23	(146)
Statement c	80	63	50	64	(459)
Statement d	7	11	19	12	(99)

V068. How often, according to your best estimates, does the publisher of your paper ask for special handling of an article about a company or organization which has some economic clout over your newspaper?

a. Never
b. Less than once a year
c. About once or twice a year
d. Several times a year
e. About once a month
f. 2-3 times a month
g. Nearly every week
h. Every week

	Publishers	Editors	Staff Members	Total	
Statement a	58%	54%	32%	48%	(320)
Statement b	10	12	18	13	(94)
Statement c	18	19	20	19	(149)
Statement d	10	11	23	14	(118)
Statement e	2	1	3	2	(16)
Statement f	1	1	3	2	(14)
Statement g	1	1	1	1	(7)
Statement h	0	0	0	0	(1)

V069. How often, according to your best estimate, does the publisher ask for special handling of an article about an organization or individual with whom he has strong social ties?
a. Never
b. Less than once a year
c. About once or twice a year
d. Several times a year
e. About once a month
f. 2-3 times a month
g. Nearly every week
h. Every week

	Publishers	Editors	Staff Members	Total	
Statement a	58%	48%	31%	46%	(302)
Statement b	8	14	10	11	(85)
Statement c	23	19	24	22	(162)
Statement d	9	16	23	16	(121)
Statement e	1	1	5	2	(21)
Statement f	1	2	4	2	(20)
Statement g	0	0	2	1	(8)
Statement h	0	0	0	0	(1)

V070. How often does the publisher ask the editor to send a reporter on a non-news mission for the company: to influence legislation, for example, or gather information on competition?
a. Never

b. Less than once a year
c. About once or twice a year
d. Several times a year
e. About once a month
f. More than once a month

	Publishers	Editors	Staff Members	Total
Statement a	90%	81%	82%	84% (612)
Statement b	7	12	10	10 (65)
Statement c	2	5	6	4 (33)
Statement d	1	2	2	2 (13)
Statement e	0	0	0	0 (0)
Statement f	0	0	0	0 (1)

V071. Do you think it is a good idea or a bad idea for a newspaper publisher to serve on the board of another local company?

	Publishers	Editors	Staff Members	Total
Good idea	11%	6%	9%	9% (73)
Bad idea	65	71	71	69 (476)
No difference	24	23	21	22 (181)

V072. (IF BAD IDEA TO V071) What if the company is non-profit, like a hospital or a symphony orchestra? Would the publisher's serving on such a board be a good idea or a bad idea?

	Publishers	Editors	Staff Members	Total
Good idea	59%	27%	21%	35% (164)
Bad idea	18	51	57	43 (205)
No difference	23	23	22	23 (105)

V073. (IF BAD IDEA TO V072) What if it was the board of a charitable enterprise like United Way or a local foundation?

	Publishers	Editors	Staff Members	Total
Good idea	27%	7%	4%	8% (21)
Bad idea	50	87	91	84 (164)
No difference	24	6	5	8 (19)

V074. (IF BAD IDEA TO V073) How about a church vestry or PTA board?

	Publishers	Editors	Staff Members	Total
Good idea	0%	5%	1%	3% (6)
Bad idea	77	38	56	49 (84)
No difference	24	57	44	48 (73)

V075. Do you think it is a good idea or a bad idea for a newspaper editor to serve on the board of another local company?

	Publishers	Editors	Staff Members	Total	
Good idea	5%	3%	3%	4%	(33)
Bad idea	80	92	88	87	(614)
No difference	15	6	9	10	(83)

V076. (IF BAD IDEA TO V075) What if the company is non-profit, like a hospital or a symphony orchestra? Would the editor's serving on such a board be a good idea or a bad idea?

	Publishers	Editors	Staff Members	Total	
Good idea	26%	10%	13%	16%	(100)
Bad idea	55	78	74	70	(418)
No difference	19	12	12	14	(92)

V077. (IF BAD IDEA TO V076) What if it was the board of a charitable enterprise like United Way or a local foundation?

	Publishers	Editors	Staff Members	Total	
Good idea	9%	2%	1%	4%	(19)
Bad idea	82	92	91	89	(363)
No difference	9	6	8	7	(33)

V078. (IF BAD IDEA TO V077) How about a church vestry or PTA board?

	Publishers	Editors	Staff Members	Total	
Good idea	11%	9%	5%	8%	(33)
Bad idea	47	48	63	53	(182)
No difference	42	43	33	39	(144)

Suppose that your paper's performance was being graded by different groups. Each year, each group would send you a report card. For each group listed, please indicate whether you would be extremely interested, very interested, somewhat interested, or not interested at all in that group's report card on your paper.

V079. Readers

	Publishers	Editors	Staff Members	Total	
Extremely	93%	87%	86%	89%	(658)
Very	6	8	12	8	(57)
Somewhat	1	5	3	2	(17)
Not	0	0	0	0	(0)

V080. Politicians

	Publishers	Editors	Staff Members	Total	
Extremely	25%	34%	27%	29%	(194)
Very	23	25	25	25	(196)
Somewhat	45	34	43	41	(300)
Not	6	6	4	5	(41)

V081. Retail advertisers

	Publishers	Editors	Staff Members	Total	
Extremely	47%	36%	29%	37%	(263)
Very	31	27	19	26	(202)
Somewhat	21	33	41	32	(231)
Not	0	4	12	5	(35)

V082. Potential investors in your company

	Publishers	Editors	Staff Members	Total	
Extremely	29%	29%	27%	28%	(193)
Very	22	17	20	19	(148)
Somewhat	25	32	32	30	(217)
Not	25	22	21	23	(163)

V083. National advertisers

	Publishers	Editors	Staff Members	Total	
Extremely	35%	31%	28%	32%	(210)
Very	37	17	15	23	(169)
Somewhat	23	40	42	35	(282)
Not	4	13	15	11	(69)

V084. People who put out other newspapers

	Publishers	Editors	Staff Members	Total	
Extremely	41%	45%	49%	45%	(315)
Very	36	31	33	33	(252)
Somewhat	21	20	18	20	(150)
Not	1	4	1	2	(13)

V085. Journalism school faculties

	Publishers	Editors	Staff Members	Total	
Extremely	24%	30%	39%	31%	(236)
Very	37	26	30	31	(234)
Somewhat	31	36	28	32	(219)
Not	8	8	4	7	(43)

V086. Security analysts

	Publishers	Editors	Staff Members	Total	
Extremely	18%	22%	17%	19%	(129)
Very	20	12	9	14	(102)
Somewhat	41	40	47	42	(309)
Not	21	26	27	25	(188)

V087. Journalism students

	Publishers	Editors	Staff Members	Total	
Extremely	21%	26%	26%	25%	(173)
Very	31	22	24	26	(179)
Somewhat	42	44	44	43	(327)
Not	6	8	6	7	(53)

V088. Classified advertisers

	Publishers	Editors	Staff Members	Total	
Extremely	42%	33%	24%	33%	(233)
Very	29	22	18	23	(181)
Somewhat	28	34	35	33	(241)
Not	1	12	23	12	(76)

V089. Your own editorial staff

	Publishers	Editors	Staff Members	Total	
Extremely	78%	81%	75%	78%	(559)
Very	19	17	20	19	(148)
Somewhat	3	2	4	3	(23)
Not	0	0	1	0	(2)

For each of the following statements, please tell me whether you agree or disagree.

V090. When there is disagreement between editor and publisher over the endorsement of a political candidate, the editor should have the final say.

	Publishers	Editors	Staff Members	Total	
Agree	22%	37%	47%	36%	(245)
Disagree	78	63	53	64	(482)

V091. An editor should not be a director or an officer of the company he works for.

	Publishers	Editors	Staff Members	Total	
Agree	16%	25%	57%	32%	(255)
Disagree	84	75	43	68	(471)

V092. It's okay for the lawyer who advises the newspaper on the legal risks it takes to sit on the company's board.

	Publishers	Editors	Staff Members	Total
Agree	65%	55%	39%	53% (392)
Disagree	35	45	61	47 (336)

V093. There are situations, like the Pentagon Papers case, where it is more loyal to the nation to violate security rules than to follow them.

	Publishers	Editors	Staff Members	Total
Agree	79%	87%	92%	86% (611)
Disagree	21	13	8	14 (114)

V094. Public concern over newspaper ethics is caused less by the things newspapers do than by their failure to explain what they do.

	Publishers	Editors	Staff Members	Total
Agree	68%	72%	60%	67% (503)
Disagree	32	28	40	33 (223)

V095. Sometimes the letters to the editor at our paper are really written by the staff.

	Publishers	Editors	Staff Members	Total
Agree	1%	0%	2%	1% (10)
Disagree	99	100	98	99 (718)

V096. An adversarial relationship between the government and newspapers is healthy for the country in the long run.

	Publishers	Editors	Staff Members	Total
Agree	78%	91%	87%	85% (606)
Disagree	22	9	13	15 (121)

V097. A state news council, modeled after the National News Council, would be a good idea.

	Publishers	Editors	Staff Members	Total
Agree	21%	29%	49%	33% (252)
Disagree	79	71	51	67 (439)

V098. A reporter who has promised confidentiality to a source should, if asked, reveal that source to his editor.

	Publishers	Editors	Staff Members	Total
Agree	91%	91%	70%	84% (595)
Disagree	9	9	30	16 (136)

Several possible "yardsticks" for evaluating newspaper companies are listed below. On a scale of 1 to 10, how important is each of these indicators to you? A score of 1 means the indicator is unimportant; a score of 10 means the indicator is extremely important.

V099. Earnings consistency

	Publishers	Editors	Staff Members	Total	
1	0%	5%	2%	3%	(10)
2	0	0	3	1	(10)
3	2	2	3	2	(16)
4	2	1	2	2	(14)
5	5	6	15	8	(68)
6	6	7	8	7	(47)
7	19	18	19	19	(116)
8	21	20	21	21	(161)
9	13	12	12	13	(85)
10	31	29	16	25	(196)

V100. Management quality

	Publishers	Editors	Staff Members	Total	
1	0%	1%	1%	1%	(3)
2	0	0	0	0	(0)
3	0	0	0	0	(1)
4	0	0	1	0	(3)
5	0	0	2	1	(6)
6	0	0	1	1	(5)
7	1	3	4	3	(25)
8	10	11	13	11	(86)
9	16	16	17	16	(126)
10	74	69	61	68	(476)

V101. Readiness to adopt new production technology

	Publishers	Editors	Staff Members	Total	
1	0%	1%	0%	0%	(1)
2	0	0	1	0	(1)
3	0	0	2	1	(4)
4	0	1	1	1	(6)
5	4	7	8	6	(42)
6	11	8	10	10	(59)
7	13	11	16	13	(100)
8	22	19	19	20	(159)
9	18	18	14	17	(126)
10	32	35	30	33	(231)

V102. Involvement with new electronic information systems

	Publishers	Editors	Staff Members	Total	
1	1%	6%	1%	3%	(8)
2	1	0	3	1	(8)
3	0	2	3	2	(12)
4	3	3	1	2	(20)
5	21	5	8	11	(71)
6	12	10	9	10	(80)
7	17	11	12	14	(104)
8	13	21	19	18	(138)
9	12	16	14	14	(107)
10	20	26	30	25	(180)

V103. Community service orientation

	Publishers	Editors	Staff Members	Total	
1	0%	1%	3%	1%	(7)
2	0	0	0	0	(2)
3	1	2	4	2	(9)
4	1	1	3	1	(11)
5	8	13	13	11	(60)
6	6	9	13	9	(63)
7	15	10	15	13	(95)
8	20	21	18	20	(151)
9	18	13	10	13	(106)
10	33	31	22	29	(225)

V104. Newspaper editorial quality

	Publishers	Editors	Staff Members	Total	
1	0%	1%	0%	0%	(2)
2	0	0	1	0	(2)
3	0	0	0	0	(0)
4	0	0	1	0	(1)
5	0	0	1	1	(6)
6	0	0	0	0	(2)
7	1	1	0	1	(8)
8	11	2	6	6	(47)
9	11	5	13	9	(78)
10	77	91	77	82	(584)

V105. Overall product quality

	Publishers	Editors	Staff Members	Total	
1	0%	1%	1%	0%	(2)
2	0	0	0	0	(1)
3	0	0	0	0	(0)
4	0	0	0	0	(0)
5	0	0	0	0	(2)

6	0	0	1	0	(3)
7	2	1	1	1	(11)
8	8	2	7	6	(48)
9	15	10	11	12	(91)
10	76	86	79	80	(571)

V106. Overall company image

	Publishers	Editors	Staff Members	Total	
1	0%	1%	1%	1%	(4)
2	0	0	1	0	(2)
3	0	0	0	0	(2)
4	0	1	1	1	(5)
5	1	4	9	5	(35)
6	5	4	7	5	(36)
7	16	16	16	16	(99)
8	29	23	17	23	(171)
9	11	15	14	13	(106)
10	37	37	35	36	(269)

V107. Financial health as represented by the balance sheet

	Publishers	Editors	Staff Members	Total	
1	1%	0%	1%	0%	(4)
2	0	0	1	0	(1)
3	0	0	4	1	(7)
4	0	1	1	1	(6)
5	2	3	11	5	(45)
6	2	5	8	5	(43)
7	14	10	17	14	(90)
8	21	31	24	26	(176)
9	24	15	12	17	(122)
10	36	35	21	31	(232)

V108. Readiness to introduce new products

	Publishers	Editors	Staff Members	Total	
1	0%	1%	5%	2%	(14)
2	0	1	3	1	(10)
3	0	1	3	1	(10)
4	0	2	3	2	(15)
5	4	7	14	8	(62)
6	4	5	7	6	(48)
7	22	15	20	19	(125)
8	20	28	17	22	(159)
9	21	18	14	18	(121)
10	28	22	14	22	(162)

V109. Readiness to expose wrongdoing

	Publishers	Editors	Staff Members	Total	
1	0%	1%	1%	0%	(3)
2	0	0	1	0	(1)
3	0	0	0	0	(1)
4	0	0	0	0	(0)
5	1	2	0	1	(11)
6	1	1	1	1	(8)
7	8	2	3	4	(27)
8	14	8	11	11	(77)
9	26	17	17	20	(147)
10	50	69	67	62	(454)

How important is *newspaper editorial quality* to each of the following goals:

V110. Helping maintain staff morale

	Publishers	Editors	Staff Members	Total	
Very Important	91%	95%	90%	92%	(679)
Somewhat Important	9	5	8	7	(50)
Not Important	0	0	2	1	(4)

V111. Helping maintain circulation

	Publishers	Editors	Staff Members	Total	
Very Important	82%	79%	62%	75%	(533)
Somewhat Important	17	21	35	24	(193)
Not Important	1	0	3	1	(7)

V112. Helping maintain service to the community

	Publishers	Editors	Staff Members	Total	
Very Important	68%	79%	70%	72%	(538)
Somewhat Important	32	20	28	26	(186)
Not Important	0	1	2	1	(9)

V113. Helping maintain advertising revenues

	Publishers	Editors	Staff Members	Total
Very Important	54%	58%	33%	49% (344)
Somewhat Important	44	37	53	44 (336)
Not Important	2	5	14	7 (53)

V114. Helping keep the public informed

	Publishers	Editors	Staff Members	Total
Very Important	93%	96%	95%	95% (689)
Somewhat Important	7	3	4	5 (42)
Not Important	0	0	0	0 (2)

Listed below are some of the things publishers do to influence editorial content. For each one, please indicate how often it happens—to your knowledge—at your newspaper.
1. Never
2. Less than once a year
3. About once or twice a year
4. About once or twice a month
5. 2-3 times a month
6. Nearly every week
7. Every week
8. Several times a week
9. Daily

V115. The publisher orders the editor to undertake a major investigation or series of articles on a specific subject.

	Publishers	Editors	Staff Members	Total
Statement 1	45%	61%	41%	50% (333)
Statement 2	24	18	22	21 (152)
Statement 3	22	18	30	23 (181)
Statement 4	8	3	5	5 (43)
Statement 5	0	0	1	0 (4)
Statement 6	1	0	1	1 (6)
Statement 7	0	0	0	0 (1)
Statement 8	0	0	0	0 (1)
Statement 9	0	0	0	0 (1)

V116. The publisher suggests a major investigation or series of articles, but leaves the final decision to the editor.

	Publishers	Editors	Staff Members	Total
Statement 1	9%	17%	29%	18% (127)
Statement 2	16	26	25	23 (157)
Statement 3	51	50	35	46 (329)
Statement 4	18	6	9	11 (79)
Statement 5	3	1	1	2 (14)
Statement 6	1	0	0	0 (4)
Statement 7	1	0	0	0 (3)
Statement 8	1	0	1	0 (4)
Statement 9	0	0	0	0 (0)

V117. The publisher demonstrates by his actions, such as public speeches, backing of causes, and civic activities what areas he would like the paper to investigate.

	Publishers	Editors	Staff Members	Total
Statement 1	64%	71%	62%	66% (450)
Statement 2	10	10	16	12 (95)
Statement 3	19	15	15	16 (123)
Statement 4	4	3	3	3 (28)
Statement 5	1	1	1	1 (10)
Statement 6	0	0	1	1 (6)
Statement 7	1	0	0	0 (2)
Statement 8	0	0	0	0 (0)
Statement 9	0	0	1	0 (2)

V118. The publisher demonstrates, by selective use of praise or criticism what he wants the editor to do.

	Publishers	Editors	Staff Members	Total
Statement 1	23%	22%	22%	22% (151)
Statement 2	6	8	11	8 (59)
Statement 3	20	27	21	23 (168)
Statement 4	27	20	19	22 (147)
Statement 5	7	11	13	11 (69)
Statement 6	7	9	4	7 (52)
Statement 7	6	2	4	4 (30)
Statement 8	4	2	1	2 (18)
Statement 9	0	1	5	2 (13)

V119. In setting ethical standards for a newspaper, which is more important for a *publisher* to do:
    a. Choosing and articulating the standards, or
    b. Choosing the right editor and trusting him to set and carry out the standards?

	Publishers	Editors	Staff Members	Total
Statement a	31%	25%	25%	27% (204)
Statement b	69	75	75	73 (513)

Listed below are some of the things a publisher might do to influence the news content of the paper. For each one, please indicate whether it is a good idea, a bad idea, or whether it is neither good nor bad.

V120. Call the desk with tips on news stories.

	Publishers	Editors	Staff Members	Total
Good idea	69%	69%	56%	65% (499)
Bad idea	12	18	24	18 (114)
Neither	19	14	21	18 (116)

V121. Catch errors in grammar and spelling and let the editor know about them.

	Publishers	Editors	Staff Members	Total
Good idea	71%	76%	48%	65% (496)
Bad idea	3	9	28	13 (86)
Neither	26	16	25	22 (147)

V122. Catch factual errors and let the editor know.

	Publishers	Editors	Staff Members	Total
Good idea	99%	95%	86%	94% (684)
Bad idea	0	1	5	2 (12)
Neither	1	4	8	4 (35)

V123. Spot stories that will offend advertisers and let the editor know.

	Publishers	Editors	Staff Members	Total
Good idea	11%	11%	3%	9% (69)
Bad idea	60	75	86	74 (524)
Neither	29	14	11	18 (138)

V124. Spot stories that will offend civic leaders and let the editor know.

	Publishers	Editors	Staff Members	Total
Good idea	10%	10%	4%	8% (67)
Bad idea	58	73	82	71 (509)
Neither	32	18	13	21 (155)

V125. Make suggestions about improving the writing in the paper.

	Publishers	Editors	Staff Members	Total
Good idea	87%	86%	63%	79% (591)
Bad idea	4	3	18	8 (48)
Neither	9	11	19	13 (92)

V126. Make suggestions about changing the design of the paper.

	Publishers	Editors	Staff Members	Total
Good idea	84%	77%	67%	76% (563)
Bad idea	1	5	8	5 (30)
Neither	14	18	25	19 (138)

V127. As closely as you can estimate, how often does the publisher of your paper walk into the newsroom?
  a. Never
  b. Less than once a year
  c. About once or twice a year
  d. About once a month
  e. 2-3 times a month
  f. Nearly every week
  g. Every week
  h. Several times a week
  i. Daily
  j. More than once a day

	Publishers	Editors	Staff Members	Total
Statement a	0%	3%	5%	3% (16)
Statement b	0	1	0	1 (4)
Statement c	4	7	13	8 (58)
Statement d	6	12	15	11 (60)
Statement e	5	13	12	10 (63)
Statement f	9	12	8	10 (58)
Statement g	4	5	3	4 (34)
Statement h	24	16	17	19 (143)
Statement i	27	15	14	19 (141)
Statement j	22	17	13	17 (145)

V128. Different newspapers have different rules for deciding what is acceptable in advertising copy. At your newspaper, how often does the publisher ask the editor's advice when a question of acceptability arises?

	Publishers	Editors	Staff Members	Total
Always	2%	6%	1%	3% (19)
Most of the time	12	8	6	9 (63)
Some of the time	35	35	14	29 (184)
Almost never	52	51	79	60 (431)

One of the topics that often comes up in the newsroom is whether a reporter with a history of personal activity in a given area is more or less qualified to cover a related field because of that history. Here are some examples, and in each one, please assume that the reporter is otherwise well qualified. Please decide whether the reporter's personal history or circumstances are likely to be a help, a hindrance, or make any difference in covering the indicated field.

V129. A reporter with a history of vigorous union activity is assigned to cover big business.

	Publishers	*Editors*	*Staff Members*	*Total*	
Help	3%	7%	19%	9%	(65)
Hindrance	75	73	63	71	(528)
No difference	22	19	19	20	(134)

V130. A black is assigned to cover civil rights.

	Publishers	*Editors*	*Staff Members*	*Total*	
Help	42%	47%	50%	46%	(305)
Hindrance	20	14	13	16	(133)
No difference	38	38	38	38	(287)

V131. An assistant city editor who has married an heiress and under-taken the task of managing her investments has been promoted to business editor.

	Publishers	*Editors*	*Staff Members*	*Total*	
Help	31%	30%	30%	30%	(215)
Hindrance	32	35	36	34	(233)
No difference	38	35	34	35	(279)

V132. A Washington bureau chief's daughter becomes secretary to a cabinet officer.

	Publishers	*Editors*	*Staff Members*	*Total*	
Help	19%	24%	22%	22%	(144)
Hindrance	31	35	33	33	(233)
No difference	50	42	45	45	(347)

V133. A reporter whose best friend is elected mayor is assigned to cover city hall.

	Publishers	*Editors*	*Staff Members*	*Total*	
Help	9%	12%	8%	10%	(75)
Hindrance	84	81	88	84	(601)
No difference	6	7	5	6	(50)

V134. A reporter whose parents run an independent oil exploration business is assigned to cover energy.

	Publishers	Editors	Staff Members	Total
Help	25%	31%	31%	28% (208)
Hindrance	41	46	42	43 (315)
No difference	34	23	28	28 (203)

V135. A copy editor whose wife runs a public relations firm sometimes edits stories which mention his wife's clients.

	Publishers	Editors	Staff Members	Total
Help	1%	1%	0%	1% (5)
Hindrance	81	74	70	75 (525)
No difference	18	25	30	24 (194)

V136. A reporter who took leave of absence to work in the vice president's successful election campaign is assigned to the Washington Bureau.

	Publishers	Editors	Staff Members	Total
Help	30%	23%	22%	25% (195)
Hindrance	56	64	66	62 (423)
No difference	14	13	12	13 (106)

V137. A reporter who was raised on a farm is assigned to cover agriculture.

	Publishers	Editors	Staff Members	Total
Help	94%	95%	94%	95% (689)
Hindrance	1	0	1	1 (4)
No difference	5	5	4	5 (34)

V138. An atheist is assigned to cover religion.

	Publishers	Editors	Staff Members	Total
Help	2%	8%	13%	8% (34)
Hindrance	69	59	50	59 (450)
No difference	29	33	37	33 (240)

V139. A reporter with a law degree is assigned to cover local courts.

	Publishers	Editors	Staff Members	Total
Help	97%	97%	94%	96% (699)
Hindrance	1	1	3	2 (11)
No difference	2	2	3	2 (18)

V140. A reporter who has served on the current mayor's staff returns to the paper to cover local politics.

	Publishers	Editors	Staff Members	Total
Help	30%	23%	29%	27% (202)
Hindrance	61	66	63	63 (439)
No difference	9	12	8	10 (78)

V141. How often does the publisher at your newspaper question or otherwise participate in the assignment of a particular reporter to a story or beat?

  a. Never
  b. Less than once a year
  c. About once or twice a year
  d. Several times a year
  e. About once a month
  f. 2-3 times a month
  g. Nearly every week
  h. Every week
  i. Several times a week
  j. Daily

	Publishers	Editors	Staff Members	Total
Statement a	46%	55%	56%	52% (367)
Statement b	21	21	20	21 (149)
Statement c	14	15	9	13 (93)
Statement d	14	6	8	10 (67)
Statement e	2	1	3	2 (17)
Statement f	1	1	2	1 (11)
Statement g	0	1	0	0 (3)
Statement h	1	0	1	1 (5)
Statement i	0	0	1	1 (5)
Statement j	0	0	0	0 (1)

V142. How often, to the best of your knowledge, does your paper publish editorial matter controlled by the business office on behalf of advertisers in the news columns (commonly known as "blurbs" or "business office musts").

  a. Never
  b. Less than once a year
  c. About once or twice a year
  d. Several times a year
  e. About once a month
  f. 2-3 times a month
  g. Nearly every week
  h. Every week
  i. Several times a week
  j. Daily

	Publishers	Editors	Staff Members	Total
Statement a	79%	76%	61%	72% (491)
Statement b	5	3	9	6 (43)
Statement c	4	5	6	5 (41)
Statement d	5	9	12	9 (74)
Statement e	2	1	3	2 (18)

Statement f	1	2	3	2	(17)
Statement g	1	2	3	2	(19)
Statement h	1	0	3	1	(10)
Statement i	0	1	1	1	(8)
Statement j	1	0	0	0	(2)

V143. As you know, some newspaper companies are privately owned, and some are at least partly owned by investors who buy and sell stock on public exchanges. Do you think that whether a company is publicly or privately owned makes any difference in the way it serves its local community?

	Publishers	Editors	Staff Members	Total	
Yes	40%	38%	39%	39%	(294)
No	60	62	61	61	(432)

V144. (IF YES TO V143) How frequently would you say the pressures of being publicly owned hinder a newspaper's ability to serve the local community: often, sometimes, rarely, or never?

	Publishers	Editors	Staff Members	Total	
Often	12%	16%	10%	13%	(40)
Sometimes	50	53	60	54	(157)
Rarely	27	19	26	24	(62)
Never	10	12	4	9	(27)

V145. Do you think that it is a good idea or a bad idea to use polls and surveys to find out what readers want to read?

	Publishers	Editors	Staff Members	Total	
Good idea	97%	92%	94%	94%	(698)
Bad idea	3	8	6	6	(31)

V146. Suppose that there were an issue that really meant a lot to the health and safety of people in your community, but people weren't very interested in it. Should the paper try to get people interested, or should it wait until their interest is aroused in some other way?

	Publishers	Editors	Staff Members	Total	
Try to get interest	100%	99%	100%	100%	(728)
Wait	0	1	0	0	(3)

V147. Suppose the issue were the effect of seat belt use in reducing deaths and injuries from auto accidents. If people aren't very interested in using seat belts, should the paper try to get them interested or wait until their interest is aroused in some other way?

	Publishers	Editors	Staff Members	Total
Try to get interest	85%	95%	87%	89% (653)
Wait	15	5	13	11 (76)

V148. Suppose the issue were the effect of diet on disease. If people weren't very interested, should the paper try to get them interested or wait until their interest is aroused in some other way?

	Publishers	Editors	Staff Members	Total
Try to get interest	89%	95%	86%	90% (662)
Wait	11	5	14	10 (67)

V149. Some newspaper people believe that every newspaper should have a written code of ethics or set of guidelines that its staff could consult when problems come up. Others say that every situation is different, and each ethical problem needs to be considered on its own merits. Which comes closest to your belief?

	Publishers	Editors	Staff Members	Total
Written code	59%	63%	63%	62% (427)
Case by case	41	37	37	38 (295)

V150. Does your newspaper have a written code of ethics or set of guidelines?

	Publishers	Editors	Staff Members	Total
Yes	55%	51%	35%	47% (319)
No	45	49	65	53 (404)

V151. (IF YES TO V150) Could you put your hands on it right now if you wanted to or would you have to look around for a while to find it?

	Publishers	Editors	Staff Members	Total
Now	78%	91%	65%	80% (242)
Have to look	22	9	35	20 (66)

Here are a few questions about people in general.

V152. Do you think most people would try to take advantage of you if they got a chance, or would they try to be fair?

	Publishers	Editors	Staff Members	Total
Most try to take advantage	9%	18%	16%	14% (112)
Most try to be fair	91	82	84	86 (615)

V153. Generally speaking, would you say that most people can be trusted or that you can't be too careful in dealing with people?

	Publishers	Editors	Staff Members	Total
Most can be trusted	86%	83%	65%	78% (558)
You can't be too careful	14	17	35	22 (169)

V154. These are two statements about ethics. Please tell me which one of them comes closest to your view:
    a. In deciding ethical questions, one should refer to certain universal truths about right and wrong which never change.
    b. There are few, if any, universal truths, and each question should be decided according to what benefits the community in the long run.

	Publishers	Editors	Staff Members	Total
Statement a	68%	68%	58%	65% (462)
Statement b	32	32	42	35 (256)

V155. How would you rate the morale in your newsroom during the past few months? On a scale of 1 to 10 with 10 being the happiest possible newsroom and 1 being the least happy, where would you put yours?

	Publishers	Editors	Staff Members	Total
1	1%	1%	5%	2% (14)
2	1	1	4	2 (15)
3	1	1	10	4 (32)
4	1	3	12	5 (41)
5	9	7	25	14 (106)
6	11	20	14	15 (98)
7	33	27	19	27 (180)
8	35	35	8	27 (192)
9	6	5	2	5 (39)
10	0	0	1	1 (5)

(EDITORS AND STAFF ONLY.)
V156. On a scale of A to F—with A being the highest grade and F being a failing grade, how would you rate the ability of your publisher to deal with ethical matters?

	Editors	Staff Members	Total
A	47%	26%	37% (169)
B	31	31	31 (159)
C	15	26	21 (92)
D	2	7	4 (25)
E	5	5	5 (25)
F	0	5	3 (15)

(PUBLISHERS ONLY.)

V157. On a scale of A to F—with A being the highest grade and F being a failing grade, how would you rate the ability of your editor to deal with ethical matters?

	Publishers	
A	64%	(136)
B	29	(68)
C	4	(10)
D	1	(4)
E	2	(5)
F	0	(1)

V158. We'd like to know how involved *you* are in civic affairs. About how many local, voluntary organizations do you belong to? Include churches, civic clubs, charitable organizations, veterans groups, and the like.

	Publishers	Editors	Staff Members	Total
Mean	7.0	2.3	1.2	3.5 (697)

V159. Now just a few questions so we'll know the kinds of people we've surveyed. In what year were you born? [Thus, age equals 1982 minus year born.]

	Publishers	Editors	Staff Members	Total
Mean age	51.4	49.2	37.4	46.1 (713)

V160. And how many years of school have you completed?

	Publishers	Editors	Staff Members	Total
Mean	16.3	15.9	15.9	16 (720)

V161. Have you ever served in the Armed Forces?

	Publishers	Editors	Staff Members	Total
Yes	69%	68%	28%	56% (396)
No	31	32	72	44 (332)

V162. (IF YES TO V161) Are you still active in the reserve?

	Publishers	Editors	Staff Members	Total
Yes	1%	3%	0%	1% (7)
No	99	97	100	99 (374)

V163. Are you black, white, or something else?

	Publishers	Editors	Staff Members	Total
Black	0%	1%	2%	1% (721)
White	100	99	97	99 (4)
Other	0	0	1	0 (2)

V164. Please indicate your sex.

	Publishers	Editors	Staff Members	Total	
Male	97%	95%	69%	87%	(627)
Female	3	5	31	13	(101)

V165. What is your religious preference?

	Publishers	Editors	Staff Members	Total	
Protestant	67%	62%	44%	58%	(429)
Catholic	13	16	23	17	(136)
Jewish	6	7	11	8	(40)
Other	4	1	4	3	(21)
None	9	14	19	14	(100)

V166. How often do you attend religious services?
   a. Never
   b. Less than once a year
   c. About once or twice a year
   d. Several times a year
   e. About once a month
   f. 2-3 times a month
   g. Nearly every week
   h. Every week
   i. Several times a week

	Publishers	Editors	Staff Members	Total	
Statement a	10%	18%	18%	15%	(92)
Statement b	12	19	19	17	(108)
Statement c	17	10	12	13	(97)
Statement d	23	15	16	18	(121)
Statement e	7	4	7	6	(48)
Statement f	10	7	7	8	(66)
Statement g	10	12	10	11	(85)
Statement h	9	14	11	11	(96)
Statement i	2	1	1	1	(12)

(PUBLISHERS ONLY.)
V167. How many years have you spent in the newspaper business?

26.5 average years   (229)

V168. Does that include any time on the news-editorial side?

Yes   66%   (144)
No   34   (79)

V169. (IF YES TO V168) How many years did you spend in news-editorial work?

15.7 average years   (141)

(EDITORS ONLY.)
V170. How many years have you spent in the newspaper business?

25.4 average years   (245)

V171. Does that include any time on the business side?

Yes   13% (32)
No   87   (211)

V172. (IF YES TO V171) How many years did you spend on the business side?

4.1 average years   (32)